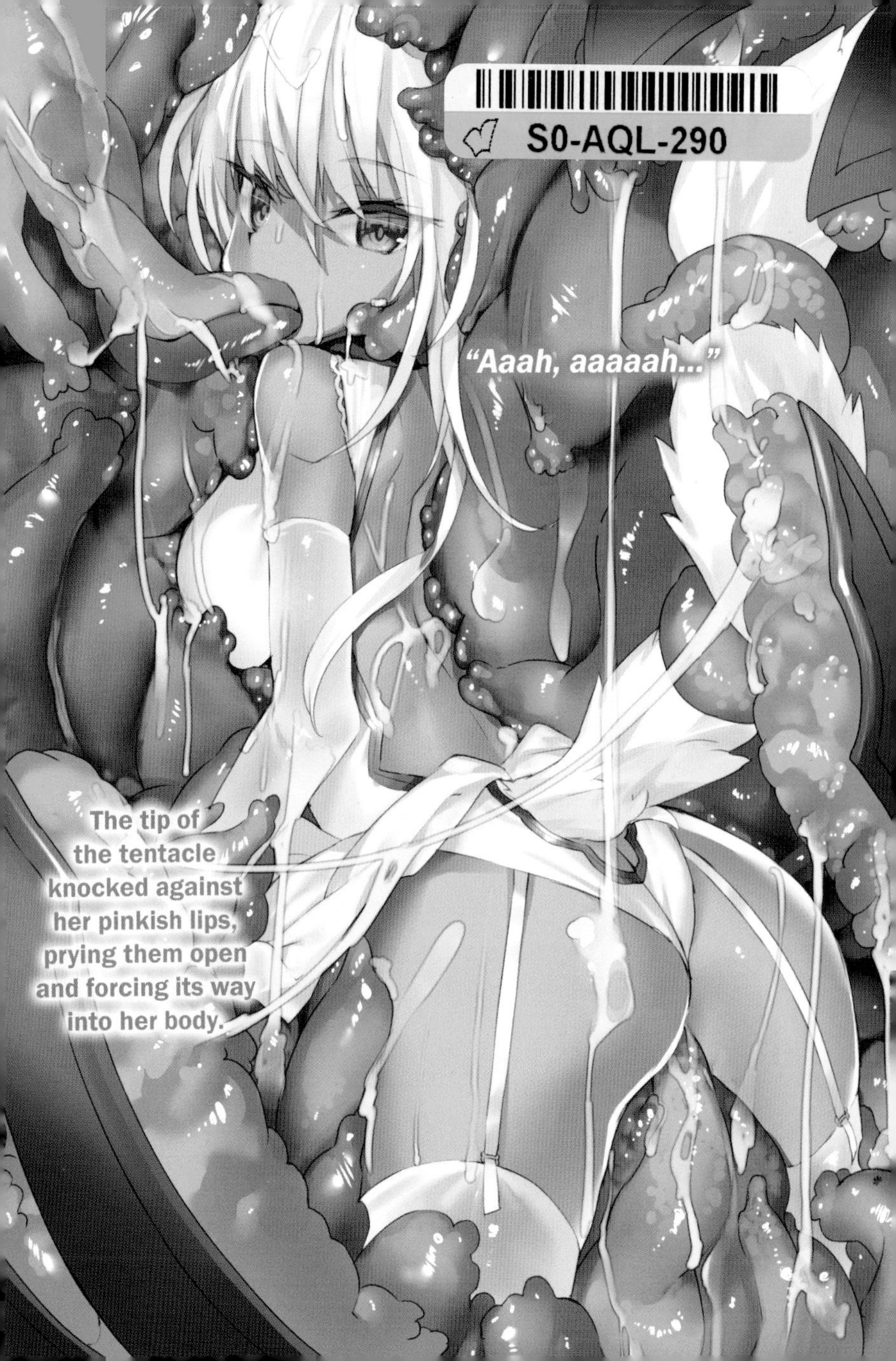

"Aaah, aaaaah..."
The tip of the tentacle knocked against her pinkish lips, prying them open and forcing its way into her body.

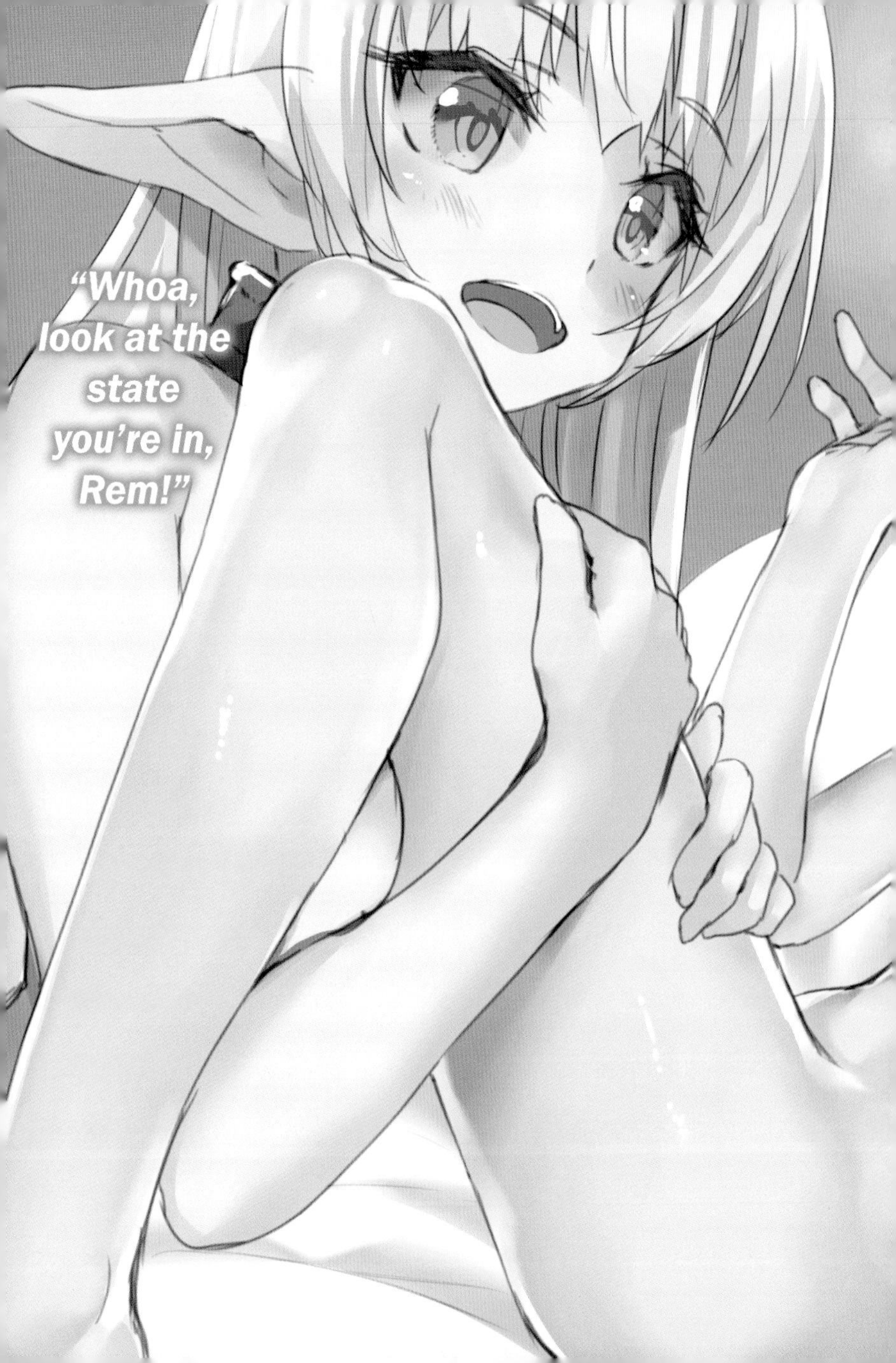
"Whoa, look at the state you're in, Rem!"

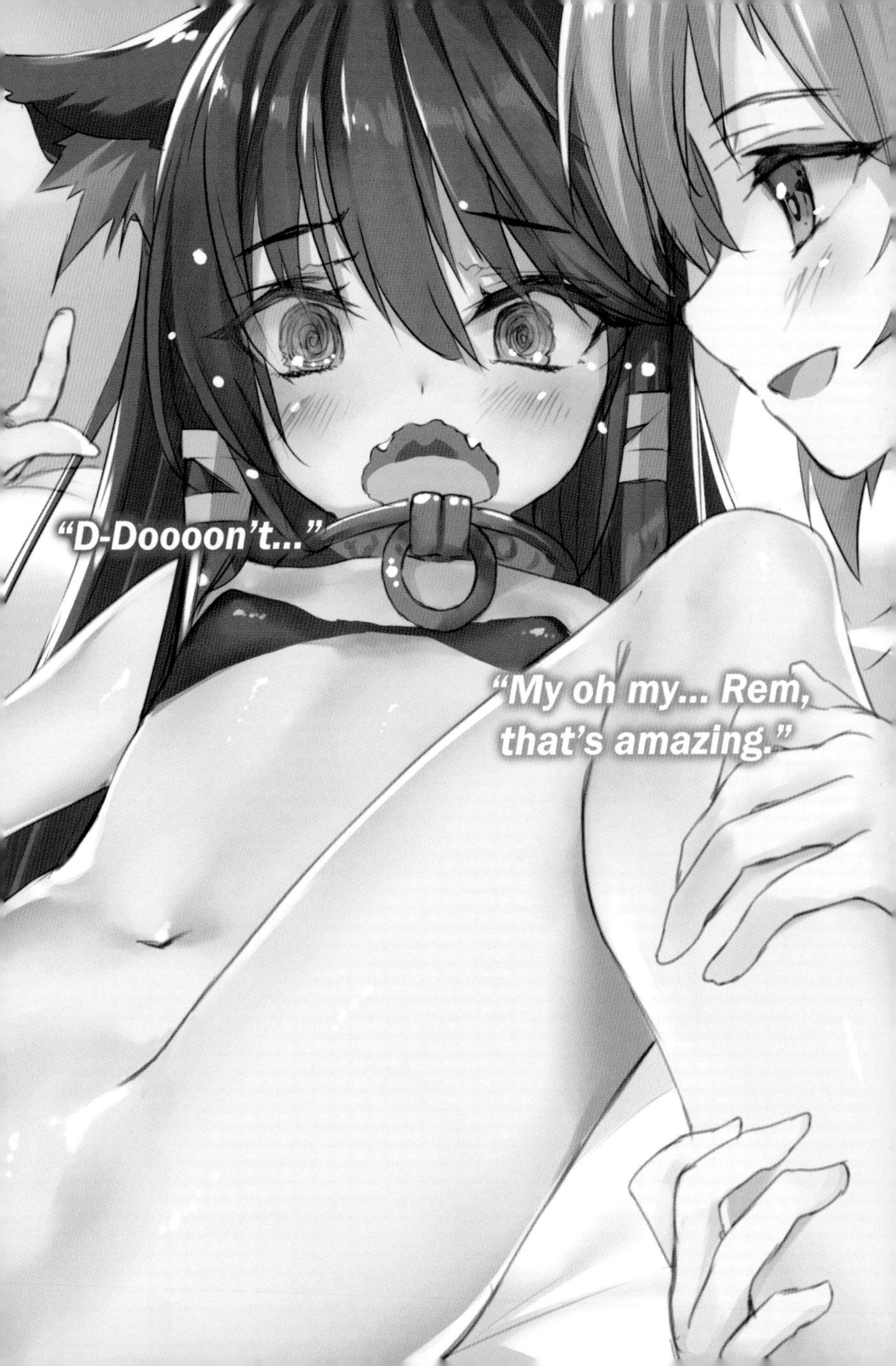
"D-Doooon't..."
"My oh my... Rem, that's amazing."

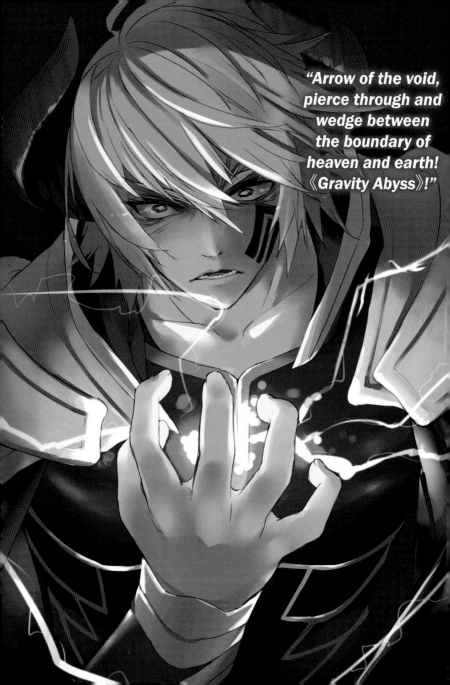

"Arrow of the void, pierce through and wedge between the boundary of heaven and earth! 《Gravity Abyss》!"

How *NOT* to Summon a Demon Lord

Demon Lord

VOLUME 12

Yukiya Murasaki

Illust. Takahiro Tsurusaki

Lumachina Weselia

The High Priest who stands as the highest authority of the church. Diablo saved her from the Cardinal Authority's devious plots, and she has worshiped him as an avatar of God ever since.

Alicia Cristela

A duke's daughter and an Imperial Knight who despises the races, despite her standing. Her objective was overthrowing the Kingdom of Lyferia, but she swore to obey Diablo to atone for her crimes.

Noah Gibun

An androgynous, handsome young man who's a duke of the highest authority in the Kingdom of Lyferia. Effectively leads the Order of Palace Knights.

A thief who had her level increased to 80 by a Subjugation Contract, but decided to study at the mage academy out of admiration for Diablo. Possesses a Holy Grail housing a level-up goddess.

Sylvie

Guildmaster of Faltra's Adventurer's Guild. Being a Grasswalker may give her the appearance of a child, but she's an experienced veteran.

Horn

A top player of a game very similar to this world. He is in fact socially inept, and can't communicate without acting the part of his in-game character. AKA: "The Demon Lord from Another World"

Diablo

Rem Galleu

A Pantherian summoner. The Demon Lord Krebskulm was sealed in her body, but she finally removed her after much hardship. Serious to a fault.

Shera L Greenwood

Princess of the Elves. Choosing Diablo as the king of her country, she finally became queen. Claims to be a summoner, but is a much more skilled archer. Speaks in a light, easygoing fashion.

How NOT to Summon a Demon Lord: Volume 12
by Yukiya Murasaki

Translated by ZackZeal
Edited by Jack Diaz
Layout by Leah Waig
English Cover & Lettering by Carl Vanstiphout

Copyright © 2019 Yukiya Murasaki
Illustrations by Takahiro Tsurusaki

First published in Japan in 2019 by Kodansha Ltd., Tokyo.
Publication rights for this English edition arranged through Kodansha Ltd., Tokyo.

Find more books like this one at www.j-novel.club!

President and Publisher: Samuel Pinansky
Managing Editor (Novels): Aimee Zink
QA Manager: Hannah N. Carter
Marketing Manager: Stephanie Hii
Project Managers: Chi Tran & Michael Meeker

ISBN: 978-1-7183-5211-7
Printed in Korea
First Printing: October 2020
10 9 8 7 6 5 4 3 2 1

contents

The Story So Far
11

Prologue
15

Chapter 1
Trying to Practice
27

Interlude
47

Chapter 2
Trying to be a Paladin Captain
55

Chapter 3
Returning to the Capital
87

Interlude
103

Chapter 4
The Capital Ablaze
118

Chapter 5
Fighting Seriously for Once
143

Epilogue
168

Afterword
172

Cover Art & Illustrations / Takahiro Tsurusaki
Design / AFTERGLOW
Editor / Satoshi Shoji

In the MMORPG *Cross Reverie*, Takuma Sakamoto was overwhelmingly powerful, and was able to role play so well that his performances were more boss-like than the actual bosses of the game. For this reason, he came to be known as the "Demon Lord."

By defeating the Demon Lord of the Mind, Enkvaros, faster than anyone else, he obtained the super rare item, the 《Demon Lord's Ring》. It was one of the ultimate pieces of equipment in the game, able to reflect all types of magic.

Then, one day, Takuma found himself summoned to a world that looked exactly like *Cross Reverie*! Having performed the ritual magic at the same time, the Pantherian, Rem, and the Elf, Shera, fought over which one of them was his Summoner. However, thanks to the Demon Lord's Ring he wore, their magic was reflected, so the Enslavement Collar meant for him clamped onto the two girls instead!

Faced with Rem and Shera arguing, Takuma was at a loss of what to do. While he may have been a superior player back in the game, he couldn't talk with other people if his life depended on it. After struggling with what to say, the words that came out of his mouth matched the Demon Lord role play he had used in the game:

"Cease your pointless squabbling. You are in the presence of Diablo."

Soon after, Diablo found himself foiling an invasion of one hundred Fallen led by a Fallen named Edelgard, as well as an attack from within the city of Faltra at the hands of the Fallen named Gregore. Diablo then found himself the recipient of a quest from the governor of Faltra, Galford. Prince Keera of the Elven Kingdom of Greenwood demanded Shera be returned to him, threatening open war with Faltra should Diablo fail to comply. The details of Galford's quest were simply to find a way to avoid the war. The bespectacled, straight-and-narrow Imperial Knight Alicia was assigned to the group as an observer to watch over their actions.

Using the 《Marionette's Flute》, Keera manipulated Shera and unleashed a forbidden Summon called the Force Hydra — yet Diablo still managed to rescue her.

After her rescue, the group set off to resurrect the Demon Lord Krebskulm trapped inside Rem. However, in the process, Krebskulm had lost a portion of her memories as a Demon Lord, being reduced to a biscuit-loving young girl who they nicknamed "Klem."

Peaceful days passed by…

Suddenly, Alicia betrayed the group! Now awakened as a true Demon Lord, Klem went into a destructive frenzy. But thanks to one of Diablo's ultimate spells and the sound of Rem's and Shera's voices, Klem was subdued and reverted to her biscuit-loving form. To ensure Klem would never go berserk again, Diablo bound her with the same enslavement magic inflicted upon Shera and Rem.

Through a string of coincidences — or perhaps God's own guidance — Diablo found himself rescuing Lumachina, a holy woman, from the Paladin Gewalt. As High Priest, Lumachina was the highest ranking member of the church. However, due to her attempts at ridding the church of corruption and avarice, she was nearly assassinated. Still seeking to reform the corrupt church, Lumachina sought the help of the Paladin Captain Batutta, setting out to meet him in Zircon Tower, which was located in the perilous expanse of the former Demon Lord's Domain. Diablo's group of adventurers accompanied her as bodyguards. After a long journey, they arrived at their destination, and were greeted by Batutta.

While there, Diablo reclaimed his own dungeon, gained many pieces of helpful equipment and items, and fought off the new Demon Lord's army, gaining new allies in the process: the Grasswalker, Horn, and the magimatic maid, Rose.

Shortly after, Horn decided to change classes and study to become a sorcerer, leaving for the magic academy.

However, they could not celebrate their victories. After being informed that the Elven king, Shera's father, had passed away, the four traveled to her homeland, where Shera was already engaged to a pig-faced Elf called Drango (for the sake of the country, of course). Diablo thwarted the wedding, giving Shera a wedding ring and assuming the throne as the new king of Greenwood.

Diablo then fought and defeated his next great opponent, the Demon Overlord Modinaram. Saving Rem, who had been taken captive by Modinaram, he gave her a wedding ring.

News of Diablo's heroic deeds reached the king of Lyferia, Delouche Xandros. Diablo attempted to ignore the order calling him for an audience with the king, but still begrudgingly found himself in the audience chamber one way or another. What awaited him in the castle wasn't words of praise, but gazes full of suspicion. Left with no choice, Diablo accepted a quest from the king as an adventurer in order to guarantee his and his companions' safety.

His quest led him to the southern frontier town of Caliture. This turned out to be Rem's hometown, and the place where her family, the Gadou Clan of martial artists, resided. There, Diablo found himself being toyed with by Rem's aunt, Solami.

"You can be confident. You're certainly a Demon Lord on this front. Nobody could compare to this overwhelming strength♥"

And so, she trained him in the use of the Glow.

The king's quest involved slaying wild beasts, but their targets turned out to be a clan of Kobolds. Being therianthropes, they were incapable of conversing with the races. But to Diablo's surprise, he found he could understand what they said.

The Kobolds saved Diablo and his group when they were stranded, even giving them food and beds to sleep in, earning a debt of gratitude with Diablo, who decided to help protect their lifestyle. However...

The governor of Caliture wouldn't budge from his decision to exterminate the Kobolds in the region, forcing Diablo to finally break away from Lyferia's army. Rem and Shera faced off once more against the Palace Knight Gewalt, but the gap in their abilities only seemed to have widened.

Rem uses the 《Demon Lord's Fang》 she previously received from Klem to become a quasi-Demon Lord, shocking Diablo by easily beating Gewalt with overwhelming power. Having exhausted her strength, Rem fell into a comatose slumber, only for Shera to shock Diablo further.

"I, uhm. I saw it. I saw what you... did in the courtyard with Solami... last night."

Prologue

Sitting at the eastern borders of the Kingdom of Lyferia was a great fortress. Situated at the bottom of a valley, its great walls blocked the winding highway. It was a vital strategic point in the eastern region of Lyferia, rivaling even the citadel city of Faltra in the west. Over the years, it had repelled countless invasions by demonic beasts and neighboring countries.

Its name was Kenstone.

Its iron gates were usually open to enable trade, but on this day they were closed shut. Atop its walls, several times the normal number of soldiers stood, their bows and spears at the ready as their expressions strained with concern and tension. Their gazes were fixed ahead, at a scarlet flag flapping in the wind.

The banner of another country.

Soldiers clad in full plate armor stood in perfect marching columns. Just the way they stood spoke volumes about how organized the army was. The commander of the citadel city of Kenstone's stationed forces, Kudanis, furrowed his mustache as he spoke.

"So, that's the Empire of Gelmed."

From the reports he'd received, they were an empire from across the sea that employed magimatic technology. All the countries in their way had already surrendered, and their forces used that momentum to further their invasion.

Lyferia's soldiers stirred. A single, fairly petite figure was walking toward the castle from the Empire's side.

"What is this, a child?" Kudanis glared in the figure's direction. "Have they sent a child as their messenger?"

None of the soldiers could answer their seasoned commander's unsolicited remark. The small figure drew closer to them, enough so that its features became clear. It removed the hood covering its head, unraveling long, silvery locks.

It was a girl. A beautiful girl with blue eyes and tanned skin. She then removed her robe, exposing a revealing outfit that looked unfit for the battlefield and which stressed her bosom, which looked neither too big nor too small. Her thighs were shapely and sensual, a longsword dangling from her waist.

Sitting on her head were triangular, fox-like ears, and a thick tail extended from her behind. She was likely a Kobold, a species that wasn't considered part of the races by the Kingdom of Lyferia and was treated as a type of animal instead.

Apparently, the Empire employs female animals as their messengers, they thought — but it wasn't so. The girl pulled the single-edged sword from her waist and declared:

"I am Aira Arjana, infantry captain of the Gelmed Empire!"

Her tone was dignified, unbefitting of her youthful appearance, and if her words were to be believed, she was none other than the commander of these invasion forces.

"Let it be known, officers and soldiers of the Kingdom of Lyferia!" She held up her sword. "Before our forces, your resistance is meaningless and futile! I do not wish for needless bloodshed. Submit at once, and open your gates!"

Unbelievably enough, the commander herself came to demand their surrender. And the commander was a woman *and* a Kobold, at that! Nothing could be more removed from the Kingdom of Lyferia's common sense. Some of the soldiers burst into laughter.

"A lady-Kobold commander?! Ahahahaha!"

Perhaps from how strained the atmosphere was, the laughter came out all the louder. Lyferia was based on the superiority of Humans, and the "role" of women was another deeply rooted prejudice of this land.

"If the Empire's armies were led by a dainty girl, how strong could they be?" Kudanis scoffed mockingly. "*The Empire is not to be feared*," he continued internally.

"Your sorcery is a century behind ours, and is no match for the Empire's might!" The fox-eared girl kept speaking, as if the sneering hadn't reached her ears. "You who know only of antiquated metal weapons ought to cease your pointless resistance. Should you surrender, we guarantee the safety of your soldiers and civilians. But if you turn your blades on us, we will meet you with punitive force and no remorse!"

"Bark on, you foolish fox!" Kudanis hollered back at her.

He was a war hero who fought alongside the last generation's hero, Alan, in the battle against the Demon Lord. He was confident and proud, knowing that no one in the kingdom could match him as a halberd wielder. Alongside Galford, governor of the eastern citadel city of Faltra, the two of them were known as the 'twin jewels' of the kingdom.

"We shall open the gates, as you wish!" Kudanis ordered grandly. "But we shan't surrender! We shall teach you the true meaning of war, you pitiful girl grasped by delusion!"

"Ooooooooooh!" The soldiers of Kenstone raised their voices.

The rings connected to the chains for opening and closing the gates were pulled by countless soldiers, causing the sturdy gates to slowly open. Aira's eyes widened in disappointment and sorrow.

"They're fighting back... I suppose there's no choice but to have them taste defeat..."

Lyferia's soldiers spilled from the opened gates, charging toward Aira.

If we kill the enemy commander, will their forces fly into a rage and charge us? Or will they lose their fighting spirit and flee? Whichever it will be, this is a chance to bring our main force to the fray and grasp victory.

Or so it would have been.

"Ooooooh!" The first wave of cavalry charged forward.

In their direct path was a single, slender girl. She may have been a skilled swordswoman, but she shouldn't have been able to fight these forces off.

Or so it should have been.

Aira bitterly clenched her teeth and swung the sword in her hands up into the air.

"Come forth... Magimatic Sol Arjanos!"

The air behind her warped. The view behind her contorted and undulated, the ripples growing bigger. From where there was previously thin air appeared a massive arm — a steel hand, clad in armor. Then a head emerged, followed by the rest of a torso.

What suddenly appeared before them was a gigantic suit of armor shining with a silvery luster.

What is that?!

Lyferia's soldiers trembled in shock, but the rushing cavaliers couldn't stop. No matter who they were up against, they had to secure victory. Even if they were up against some kind of massive magical beast, these high level cavaliers' 《Lance Charge》 would inflict effective damage.

Aira floated into the air slightly, as if drawn to the suit of armor. She squeezed her eyes shut, and then...

"Connect!"

The next moment, the chestpiece of the massive suit of armor opened, and with a slimy noise, countless tentacles spurted out from within it. Those tentacles, which looked strikingly similar to viscera, coiled around Aira's scantily dressed body with a wet sound.

They twined around her slender waist and crawled under her clothes, forcibly forcing her legs open.

"Nnng…" Aira clenched her teeth as she felt a shiver run down her spine.

One long tentacle rubbed against her pelvis from behind with sliding motions.

"Aaah, aaaaah…"

The tip of the tentacle knocked against her pinkish lips, prying them open and forcing its way into her body.

"Haaaa… Nnng…"

Sticky, yellowish threads came out of the tip of the tentacle inside her. Those fine, thin threads coiled around Aira's nerves, spreading throughout her body and eventually reaching her brain. It looked like the giant armor was devouring her, trying to physically consume her.

But even in the face of this unusual sight, Lyferia's cavaliers didn't stop their charge. If anything, they only strode faster.

The chestpiece of the Magimatic Sol Arjanos closed. Some of the tentacles failed to slither back in time, and after being caught in the gaps of the armor, fell to the ground, spewing out white, sticky fluids. Arjanos' eyes lit up in a bluish-white glow.

"Ooooh…"

That same light emitted from the armor's gaps and then its joints. It was visible at a glance that this was the glow of magic.

†

"Aaaaaaaaaaaah!" Lyferia's cavalry unleashed mighty thrusts at the armor.

These were strikes that would pierce even the heart of a giant many times the size of a man. But a high-pitched metallic sound echoed, and the tips of the cavaliers' magically enhanced lances were repelled by the armor.

"Whaaaaat?!" The knights' eyes widened in shock.

"Oooooooooooooooooooooooooh!" Arjanos swung its hand into the air.

The next moment, a massive single-edged sword, longer than the height of an adult, appeared out of thin air.

With each swing of its blade, Arjanos sent soldiers flying through the air, reducing their numbers considerably. The knights, meanwhile, surrounded their massive opponent and tried to attack it from behind, but their enchanted lances failed to inflict any kind of damage on it. The moment before the blades struck the armor, they were pushed back, as if repelled by an invisible wall.

"Haaaaaaaaaaaa!" Arjanos' blade began emanating a bluish light.

Its already intense slashes grew even stronger, and faster at that. The battlefield rapidly became littered with the soldiers' corpses.

It was all too overwhelming.

But it was then that someone appeared on the battlefield. A man clad in armor emblazoned with an insignia in the shape of a flame.

"My men... How dare you, you monster...!"

It was Lyferia's commander, holding a golden halberd in hand — Kudanis. He faced off against Arjanos, which stood covered in the blood splatter of its foes. Lyferia's soldiers regained their zeal, cheering him on from atop the walls.

"Kudanis! Kudanis! Kudanis!"

But Gelmed's soldiers raised their voices too, as if to match them.

"Bastenia Ra Aira! Bastenia Ra Aira!"

They chanted, in their tongue, words that roughly meant, "Victory to Lady Aira."

"Your weapons cannot hope to break through the protection of the Magimatic Sol." Aira's muffled voice spoke from within the armor's chestpiece. *"This cannot even be called a war. Forfeit this battle."*

It seemed Aira hadn't been devoured by the armor, but was rather wearing and manipulating it. It was fearsome magic.

So this is magimatic technology... Kudanis thought in admiration.

It seemed her claims that the Empire was a century ahead of Lyferia weren't mere exaggeration. Still, Kudanis tightened his grip on his halberd, refusing to back down.

"Do not look down on us, you brat... The Lyferian army has fought the Demon Lord time and again! Regular weapons not being effective is not enough to shake us."

"The Demon Lord has appeared in the Empire of Gelmed already... it was not that great of a threat."

"Cease your bluffing..."

"If the Demon Lord is supposed to rival God, perhaps it means Gelmed's magimatic technology surpasses even God Himself. Not that I've ever seen any kind of God before."

"Arrogant fool. I shall... beat you, along with your conceit, up to the heavens themselves!"

"You try to challenge a Magimatic Sol with a primitive weapon like a halberd... and you call me conceited?"

Aira sighed and raised Arjanos' blade. Kudanis didn't change his posture. A sword larger than his entire body fell down on him from above, which he caught with his golden halberd. Aira and the Empire soldiers expected him to be split in half along with his weapon.

But with fluid motions one would never have expected from his brusque appearance, Kudanis warded off the blade, and with that same momentum, revolved his halberd. Flames blew out of its tip, and that turning motion turned into a sharp thrust, aimed at Arjanos' breastplate!

But while Aira thought it would be deflected before it even struck the armor, once again, her expectations were betrayed. The golden halberd pierced Arjanos' armor, cracking its silvery shell and sending fragments of metal flying about.

"You penetrated the barrier…?!"

Kudanis pulled back his halberd and once again fixed his stance.

"The martial art 《Spiral Flame Spear》 returns the damage of any attack it blocks to the aggressor. How do you like the taste of your own attack?"

"To think such a technique exists… I will admit I didn't expect it, but your greatest failure is that you couldn't finish me off with that surprise attack. You likely can't use that technique unless you have a blow to reflect."

"Hmph…" Kudanis scoffed, his lips curling unpleasantly.

Like Aira said, the fact he couldn't finish her off was a bitter failure. The moment the halberd's tip made contact, Arjanos pulled back, making the thrust that much more shallow. Kudanis realized he'd misjudged his opponent.

A wonderful reaction... This is not just this Magimatic Sol's abilities, the lass inside it is just as skilled.

The two stared each other down. Aira didn't carelessly attempt an attack, knowing it would be again deflected by the halberd and directed back at her. Arjanos cautiously held up its single-edged sword, standing still.

Kudanis charged forward. He stopped when she expected him to move, and moved when she expected him to stop — a truly seasoned veteran. But Aira was experienced herself, and didn't do anything as foolish as hurriedly swinging her sword. She blocked Kudanis' attack with her left arm, seeking the right moment when the halberd wouldn't be able to deflect her.

But the halberd then lit up with a blinding flash.

"《Smiting Rage Slash》!"

Arjanos' armor shattered and its massive left arm fell to the ground with a thud.

"How?!" Aira screeched.

"It is time you realize, girl!" Kudanis grinned. "Piercing absolute defense is but a part of the basics! There are battlefields out there where one can only be considered of use if they're capable of penetrating any and all defenses!"

"You destroyed a barrier without any magimatic weapons... And you call me a monster?!"

"Too slow!"

His next attack was unleashed. Arjanos retreated, trying to create space between the two of them. It was unable to evade, and was gouged along its flank. Silvery fragments scattered in the air. A red, blood-like fluid seeped out of the points where the armor had broken away, except it didn't smell like blood, but rather like oil and sulfur.

Arjanos swept with its sword, trying to drive away Kudanis' assault, but its blow was deflected by the halberd.

"Sloppy once you're on the back foot, eh, girl?! Your lack of experience in fighting powerful opponents is your undoing!"

The halberd spewed fire as part of its Spiral Flame Spear martial art, soaring toward Arjanos' chestpiece. It was then that an arrow of light struck down on them from the heavens.

†

Kudanis narrowly evaded the arrow, but a second one flew in his direction as if in pursuit, stabbing into the ground.

"Ugh…?!" Kudanis retreated, staggering a few steps back.

Another Magimatic Sol flew down toward them. Unlike Arjanos, its armor was a deep crimson color, and its outer details were a bit different, but it seemed to be a similar model to Aira's Magimatic Sol.

"*Lady Airaaaaaaaa!*" A girl raised her voice from inside it. "*Aaaah?! There's a hole near Arjanos' hatch! Lady Aira! Lady Aira!*"

"*I'm fine, Erina…*"

"*Aaaah… Thank goodness!*"

And then came another unit, this time colored white.

"*Captain! I apologize for my tardiness!*"

"*You've come, Rikka.*"

"*Yes. I'm so glad I made it…*"

As Rikka heaved a long sigh, Erina scolded her.

"*You didn't make it in time, you dumb-dumb! Your sucky piloting almost cost Lady Aira her life!*"

"*Uuu… I'm sorry.*"

"No..." Aira smiled wryly. "*Command demanded a reckless operation out of us. You both did well just by coming here as fast as you did. Could you lend me your aid?*"

"*E-Erm, Arjanos seems to be severely damaged, so leave this to us!*"

"*I would love to take you up on that offer, but we can spare no effort against an enemy like this. He has techniques capable of penetrating a Magimatic Sol's barrier.*"

Those words elicited shocked responses from Erina and Rikka.

"*Huh?! With that primitive weapon?!*"

"*Whoa... There really are all sorts of techniques we've never seen before across the sea.*"

"*Rikka, let's attack him from both sides. Erina, cover us with your magimatic bow.*"

""*Roger, ma'am!*""

Arjanos' movements hadn't grown any slower, and it propped up its sword. The white Magimatic Sol, holding up a large shield, closed in on Kudanis. He kept his gaze fixed on both targets, but balls of light were already flying toward his legs.

I will die here... Kudanis steeled himself. *But I won't die in vain.*

He threw his golden halberd at the white Magimatic Sol. This blow was his ace in the hole.

"Get crushed, you monster!"

"*Aaaah?!*"

Rikka blocked it with her large shield. It didn't pierce through it. It got through the barrier, but the shield even blocked Kudanis' greatest blow. There likely wasn't any attack that could break through that shield in all of Lyferia.

With Kudanis bare-handed, Arjanos bore down on him with its single-edged sword.

"Prepare yourself!"

"Hmph… To win the war, one must finish off the enemy's commander."

Kudanis caught the blade with his left arm, shifting away the attack as if it were a halberd. But it wasn't such a sturdy weapon, so his arm was crushed, the flesh tearing off and the bone shattering.

It was a Spiral Flame Spear that used his own body — and its aim was fixed on Arjanos' already broken breastplate.

"Your head is mine!"

"Lady Aira?!" Erina screamed.

At that moment, Arjanos' breastplate swung open. From within it appeared Aira, her own single-edged blade in hand.

"I retract my assessment of you being powerless. You were, without a doubt, a fearsome opponent."

She swung her blade, cutting through Kudanis' abdomen. His fist had connected with Arjanos, but the slash sent him flying back.

Kudanis met his demise at the hands of the "frail" girl he made light of, while Aira lost her unit to the man whose resistance she deemed to be "futile."

Putting her sword back into its scabbard, Aira turned her eyes to the citadel city. With its heroic general gone, the soldiers were struck with fear. Now would be a prime time to attack, but…

"Erina, Rikka, are you all right?"

"Why, of course I am."

"I think my shield got a little cracked…"

"We lost a Magimatic Sol on our first battle… Was I too fixated on achievement? We should wait for Migurtha to arrive. Though I don't see the situation of the war changing any by the time they do…"

And just as Aira predicted, soon enough a white flag fluttered above the citadel city of Kenstone.

In the depths of the Kobolds' tunnels, it was hard to tell if it was day or night, but it was likely a bit before dawn. Rem was still sound asleep. When she had lost her clothes before, she had materialized replacement clothes using the Glow. However, these were gone since she was unconscious, meaning she was stark naked. They covered her up in a blanket so she wouldn't be cold.

Her breathing was calm and her body temperature seemed to be in order. She was likely just exhausted, and would eventually wake up on her own accord.

Diablo was seated next to Rem.

"When Rem gets better, we should head back to the capital. Leaving Horn and Sylvie there might be dangerous."

Shera was next to him. She had also been injured while fighting a mighty opponent, but was all better now thanks to a recovery potion he'd given her.

"So we go back with Horn and Sylvie to Faltra?"

"Yeah, and after that…"

They take Klem and run off to Greenwood? But that presented a major problem: there were no biscuits in Greenwood.

"…Well, I'll figure out the rest later. First we need to get to the capital. Just getting in will be a challenge."

"Maybe we can ask Lumachina."

"Mm?"

"And Alicia's in the capital, too."

"Her, huh… No, at this point, we should make use of all the connections we have."

"Erm…"

Shera suddenly brought her face closer to his. He'd gotten used to seeing her, but having her all-too-beautiful face so close to his still made a blush creep over his cheeks. That was one habit he'd likely never get over.

"Wh-What, Shera?"

"I, uhm. I saw it."

"Huh?"

Shera blushed.

"I saw what you… did in the courtyard with Solami… last night."

Shera formed a small ring with her fingers and brought her pink lips to it. It had happened the other night, when Diablo and his group stayed with Rem's family, at the Gadou clan's estate. The family head was the younger brother of Rem's father (her uncle), who was away on some expedition. It was instead managed by his younger sister Solami (Rem's aunt), who served as assistant instructor.

Solami had a very uninhibited personality, and did some acts in the courtyard with Diablo that could only be collectively described as 'this and that', which were overall a huge ruckus…

Shera saw that?!

Diablo felt himself break into a cold sweat as his Demon Lord role play crumbled away.

"Aaah… Uuu…" Diablo stammered.

"There it is again." Shera cocked her head curiously. "You do this thing sometimes where you start saying 'aaah' and 'uuu'."

Well, excuse me for having a communication disorder!

In his original world, Diablo was an introverted, shut-in gamer, and talking to drop-dead gorgeous girls was completely unthinkable for him. Even just nodding when the cashier at the convenience store asked him if he wanted his food microwaved was a herculean task, and whenever they got his change wrong he could only silently accept it and go back home depressed.

But when he played the role of a Demon Lord in the game, Diablo could speak to people directly. That was just what a Demon Lord would do, after all.

And for that matter, a Demon Lord wouldn't be fussed over being caught in the act, either! And with that, the Demon Lord role play switch in Diablo's brain flipped over to 'on'.

"Are you interested in the Glow too?"

"Gloo?"

"Adventurers call it SP, but Rem's family, the Gadou clan, call it the Glow. They have a much wider range of applications for it, though."

"So that's how Rem became so strong all of a sudden?!"

"There might be something else at play there, but... She did use the Glow, yes."

Diablo didn't know the reason Rem had become a quasi-Demon Lord. She never did tell him that Klem had given her the 《Demon Lord's Fang》.

"Ooh, so that's called the Glow." Shera nodded, seemingly convinced.

"Warrior classes naturally use their SP for martial arts, but it's even more important for grapplers, since they don't use weapons."

At least, that's what Diablo knew from *Cross Reverie*, but that logic still seemed to apply in this world.

"I know a few, too."

"Archers use martial arts too, after all."

"Except I'm a summoner!"

Being Elven royalty, Shera was born with innate talent as an archer. But when she decided to become an adventurer, she found she didn't like to spend her nights all alone in the wilderness, and became a summoner for that reason... She still chose to continue down that path after gaining companions, but since she hadn't been training her skills as a sorcerer, she was likely still level 30. She always did use her bow, after all.

In *Cross Reverie*, classes were fixed. One could distribute their bonus class points freely, but gaining levels in multiple classes wasn't possible. If one wanted to try a different class, they'd have to make a different character (which cost real life money).

But this world was different. Diablo was an elemental sorcerer, but also gained levels as a warrior, which made him realize something: maybe the rules regarding leveling up multiple classes didn't come from *Cross Reverie*, but from some other game.

There was another game run by the same developer — a smartphone-based social game called *Girls' Arms* — where characters would gain weapon experience points depending on what weapons they had equipped. For example, equipping swords gave experience for melee combat, while equipping a gun increased ranged combat skills.

Diablo had no way of being sure, but that theory did make everything make sense. In other words, if he wanted to raise his level as a summoner, he'd have to fight using summons. The logic behind it wasn't clear. Maybe it had something to do with how one's state of mind changed depending on the weapon they used, which connected to what levels one gains?

Incidentally, Diablo previously had a staff called the ⟪Tonnerre Empereur⟫, which could take the shape of a sword, but it fell under the category of a magic staff, which meant it didn't gain him any experience in melee combat.

Solami did smash it, though...

It was a painful loss, since it was an EX-class piece of equipment that was useful even for fighting Demon Lords. Diablo collected items, so he had countless weapons stored away, but only a handful of them were upgraded to their maximum strength. He did have a weapon in his pouch, the ⟪Seraphix Sword⟫, but only because it had an effect that increased his experience points gain. It wasn't suited for fighting powerful enemies.

He'd eventually have to go back to his base to get another weapon, it seemed.

†

"So does the Glow have anything to do with what you did with Solami?" Shera's voice dragged Diablo out of his thoughts.

"O-Oh, yes... Of course. That was training for using the Glow."

That wasn't a lie. Compared to how adventurers used martial arts, the Gadou clan's applications of the Glow were far wider, and what they did that night did give him a glimpse into that.

"I wanna learn how to use it, too!" Shera said, her eyes sparkling.

"H-Hmm... Very well. When we get the chance."

"I wanna learn how to use it *now*!"

"Right now?!"

"I mean, I... I lost again." Shera drooped her shoulders.

Diablo hadn't been there to witness the fight, but the Kobolds did tell him. Shera and Rem had fought the Palace Knight Gewalt's summon beasts. Judging by the Kobolds' descriptions, they'd fought 《Fafnir》 and 《Efreet》. Both were limit-broken, SSR-class summons, which stood as a testament to Gewalt's skills.

Shera was likely on the brink of breaking the level limit as an archer — she was either level 99, or very close to it. But the difference in combat experience had decided the match.

"If I was stronger, the Kobolds wouldn't have had to fight and Rem wouldn't have had to go all crazy-like." Shera said, her expression uncharacteristically serious.

"Perhaps."

"And I wouldn't have had to run away from my brother... or say goodbye to you like I did."

"That wasn't your fault."

"But you and Rem are always protecting me..."

That's not true.

Compared to how she was when he'd first met her, Shera was a true, proper adventurer. With the gear Klem had strengthened, she was more than a match for any low-ranking Fallen. But Gewalt was simply out of her league.

Besides, it's not like I've mastered the Glow, either.

"C'mon, teach it to me too, Diablo! What should I do? Should I lick your belly button?" Shera stuck out her tongue and wiggled its tip.

Solami wasn't licking my belly button back there... Diablo winced.

But he couldn't explain it to her and expect her to understand. Shera, in the meanwhile, undid her belt and lifted the hem of her one piece dress, revealing everything from her white panties to her well-shaped navel.

"Or maybe you need to lick my belly button? Will that make me stronger?"

"Agaaaaaagaaah...?!"

With that kind of sight before his eyes, Diablo's composure went out the proverbial window.

If you let me lick your belly button you'll get superpowers~

Diablo couldn't say something like that when she was so earnestly worried about it, though. Diablo crossed his arms, perplexed. Even with Shera's navel and panties exposed before him, ruminating over what it was that would help her become stronger made him focus inward and forget about everything around him.

"...Back then, Solami used her Glow and had me touch her so she could guide me on how to sense it. Maybe we can try that?"

"Alright!" Shera lowered the hems of her one-piece dress' skirt and nodded.

"I think you'd be better off being trained by Solami instead."

"Would she teach me if I asked?"

"No..."

There was something he hadn't told Shera. As the Gadou clan's assistant instructor, Solami was given a job by Caliture's governor — to keep Diablo from going to help the Kobolds. He'd had no choice but to fight her, and unleash spells so powerful she wasn't able to get back on her feet.

And now Diablo and his group had broken away from the Kingdom of Lyferia and were wanted individuals. So what was Diablo to do now, go back to the frontier city Caliture and ask the person who almost punched a hole through his stomach to teach him the secrets of her clan? That just wouldn't fly, even with Rem's family.

Diablo stuck out his finger. He wasn't as used to this as he was to using elemental magic, but…

"I'll use the Glow. This is a martial art to increase the body's strength using SP. Try sensing it."

"I'll try my hardest!"

Diablo had to try his hardest, too. Sasara the swordmaster taught him how to use martial arts in conjunction with wielding weapons, but using the Glow required maintaining a far more gentle, subtle balance.

To make an analogy, what Sasara had taught him was how to heat up a TV dinner, while Solami preached the method of how to make a full meal, down from the base ingredients. Among many adventurers, martial arts spread as an easy-to-use way to get stronger, but mastering the Glow would allow one to adapt to more situations.

The Glow built up within Diablo's body. And as Diablo extended his finger, Shera…

"Om."

…plopped his finger into her mouth. The wet, soft sensation of her tongue brushed against his finger as heat built up in her body.

"Wh-What?" Diablo stiffened.

"Mha… I'm supposed to put it in my mouth, right? Like this? Or this?"

She did see Solami put something in her mouth, after all. The sensation of her small tongue sent tingles running down Diablo's spine. His heart was beating like a drum.

I can't tell her what just touching my hand would do at this point.

He wasn't in the state of mind to concentrate on the Glow anymore. If anything was concentrating, it was his blood, rushing to his lower half.

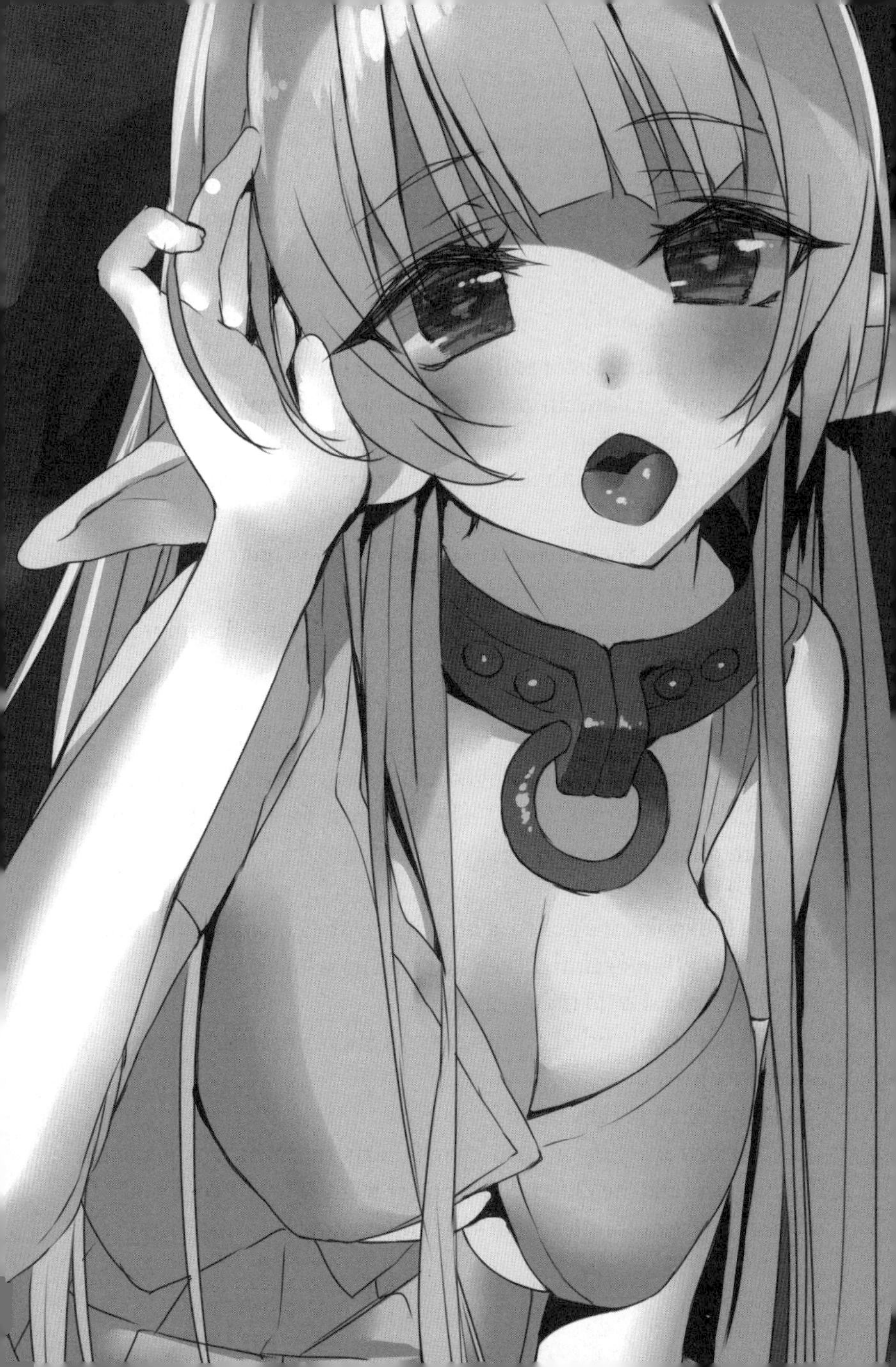

"Mmm?!" Shera's eyes widened.

"Wh-What is it?!"

"I can feel it! I can tell, Diablo! That's the Glow, right?! I can see it gathering down there!"

"……"

She can see it…

But that aside, Shera really was a genius. When Diablo had first touched on the Glow, all he could feel was Solami's boobs, and it took her forcibly using the Glow to manipulate his body for him to tell. In the end, he'd only learned how to use it by feeling it within his own body.

"Amazing!" Shera seemed excited. "This is incredible! I never knew you could use SP like this!"

"Y-Yes. So you saw it. Not bad," he said, giving the impression he was better than her.

But he was actually shocked. Even if Shera, an archer, was more used to using SP than Diablo, an elemental sorcerer, this was impressive. At this rate, she might be able to use the Glow very soon.

"Diablo, show me more." Shera leaned forward. "Something stronger, please."

"H-Hmm."

As she spoke, she poked at his finger with her tongue, disturbing his ability to think calmly. Then he came up with an idea.

"Next you should try it yourself."

Diablo finally pried his finger from Shera's mouth. It was warm and swollen.

"Huh? Can I really do it?"

"Archers use SP for their martial arts too, which is what the Gadou clan calls the Outer Glow. So try using it inside your body, to up your physical abilities. That's the Inner Glow."

He proudly repeated Solami's explanation. Relating secondhand information smugly like he knew it all was something he should feel ashamed of, but… there wasn't much to do given the situation. A Demon Lord couldn't say "Solami taught me that…" It would ruin his dignity.

"Okay, let me try! Here."

Shera extended her finger.

"Mm?"

"It's your turn to suck now. I'll try using the Glow."

"N-No, uhh…"

There's no point to me sucking on your finger? You'll be able to tell by yourself if you use the Glow.

But Shera simply extended her finger with a face utterly free of doubts. Diablo was perplexed. Should he just go ahead and plop it in his mouth? No, maybe he should refuse and explain that there's no need for this? But she is concentrating wholeheartedly on the Glow, so maybe he should just play along?

It was then that Shera exclaimed in understanding.

"Oh, so fingers don't work for beginners?!"

"Huh?"

"Right, she was licking your belly button, Diablo…"

"…Ah, yes…"

Except it wasn't his belly button.

"Here!"

Shera raised her skirt again, revealing her navel and panties again.

Is she telling me to lick it?! Diablo froze in place.

"….Rrrrg!"

It was then that they felt something like a tremor beside them.

"What in the *world* are you two doing?!"

37

Diablo jolted and turned his gaze, as did Shera, who was still holding up her clothes.

"Rem?!"

Rem looked at them with a wide-eyed, furious expression that made her look like she might turn into a Demon Lord right then and there.

"…And while I was sleeping right there next to you."

"It's Rem, Rem, Rem, it's really Rem!" Shera clung to her in a hug.

"Wha?! What's gotten into you…"

"That way you get angry! It's really you, Rem!"

"…If you know I'm angry, please let go of me."

"I was so scared earlier!"

Diablo recalled what had happened a short while ago. Rem had become a Demon Lord and gave off clear bloodlust, enough to make Diablo shudder. He recalled how her eyes glinted red as she said, "…I wish to kill you… and then myself." How her spear of Glow, powerful enough to defeat Efreet, aimed at his heart.

He thought he was going to die.

Thank heavens I'm still alive…

Given his lack of social skills, Diablo never expected to be on the receiving end of a girl's murderous rage.

Wait, that's not right.

It was *exactly because of* his lack of social skills that he'd ended up on the receiving end of a girl's murderous rage. If he was some normie chad, he would've been able to handle even two or three girls no problem. But it was his lack of ability to say the right, considerate words when they were needed most that made others anxious, sad, and disappointed, resulting in sunken relationships.

"Forgive me." Diablo said to Rem.

"Ah…"

"I am a Demon Lord. I probably am not up to your expectations."

"N-No… I got angry on my own, and… When I used the Demon Lord's Fang Klem gave me, I, well, I lost my sense of reason…"

"Hm?"

A Demon Lord's Fang? There was no item like that in Cross Reverie.

From how Rem described it, it made one lose their sense of reason, but caused their stats to skyrocket.

"…It's not Klem's fault." Rem explained. "She was trying to keep me alive in her own way, out of concern. I only went berserk like I did because of my own weakness."

"Let's become strong together, okay?" Shera said, hugging her tightly. "I'll work really hard, so…"

"…You're right. Next time, let's beat Gewalt with our own power. I have my own pride to consider, after all. I can't afford to lose to the same opponent a third time."

"Right!"

The two exchanged a glance and smiled. Diablo pondered pathetically to himself that Rem seemed to smile so much more around Shera than when she was around him.

Man… Talking to people sucks…

†

Rem put on the clothes the Kobolds left for her. Unlike the furs they always wore, these were normal clothes worn by the races. Namely, it was a native garb worn by the people of the south. Apparently they had traded with some people of the races for it.

"…These are nostalgic." Rem looked down at her outfit. "I used to wear clothes like this when I was little."

"They look good on you!" Shera complimented her.

See, that's the kind of thing that never seems to come out of my mouth. Diablo scratched his head awkwardly.

"…Diablo, about our next course of action," Rem began.

"Hmm."

It was about time they switched gears.

"…I assume we've broken off from the Kingdom of Lyferia."

"Is Gewalt still alive? How did he report this to Caliture's governor? How did the king take the news? There's still too much we don't know, but it's safe to assume we'll be pursued," Diablo stated.

Rem nodded.

"…I assumed this day would come, sooner or later."

It was bound to happen, given his tendency to declare that he's a 'Demon Lord'.

"But, but!" Shera shook her head. "If the other option was abandoning the Kobolds, I'd rather be pursued!"

"…Right you are."

Some things are more important than just loss and gain.

"First we head for the capital. Depending on how Lyferia acts, we need to make sure Sylvie and Horn are safe."

"…We should hurry."

Rem rose to her feet, but then staggered a little.

"Shouldn't you rest a bit longer?"

"…I'll be honest, my arms and legs hurt quite a bit. It's probably recoil from using the Glow too much… I can still walk though. I won't be a burden to you."

Usually, Rem would insist she was fine even if she wasn't, so hearing her admit she was unwell was a surprise. The pain she was going through was likely enough to make a normal person scream and writhe.

Still, time wasn't on their side.

"Leave all the monsters along the road to me." Diablo nodded. "Just concentrate on walking."

"Understood."

Bidding the Kobolds farewell, Diablo and his group left the forest before dawn.

†

When they found their way back to the highway, the sun was already at its peak.

"Ugh…" Shera whined. "I'm starving…"

"…We should be thankful we still have some water."

The Kobolds offered to let them take some food for the trip, but they declined. Their whole clan was facing a great migration, and no amount of preserved food would be enough. The Kobolds said they were grateful to still have their lives, but Diablo couldn't burden them any more.

"Hey, isn't that an inn town?" Shera pointed down the road.

"…So it seems. But would approaching it really be safe?"

If word of their revolt had already spread, they would likely be pursued by militia and sentries.

"I don't care if they catch us… I want food…" Shera said, forlornly rubbing her belly.

"…Your strength of will is lacking."

"If anyone dares oppose us, we need only eliminate them." Diablo shrugged. "Perhaps finding out here whether we're wanted or not would make things simpler in the future."

"…True."

He said 'eliminate', but he didn't want to have to fight the races, at least so long as they weren't villainous scum. He needed to come up with a way for them to get some food without hurting anyone.

They approached the town only to find a carriage sitting in the middle of the road. They tried to pass it by when someone descended from its wagon: a Pantherian with a cat's head.

"Young miss!"

It was one of the Gadou clan's disciples, and one of the more striking, prominent ones. Diablo steeled himself. This man and the clan cherished Rem, but felt even more strongly for their assistant instructor, Solami. Diablo had defeated her, but doubted she'd died…

He stood before the cat-headed Pantherian. Rem seemed to be thinking the same thing as she hesitated to step forward.

"…Ambushing us, Houzen?"

Apparently that was his name.

"I've been waiting for you, young miss!" Houzen raised both hands into the air, trying to signal he meant them no harm.

Still, they couldn't be careless. These ancient martial artists had techniques that allowed one to spring from a stance of submission straight into an offensive position.

"…I heard Diablo and Auntie fought," Rem said.

"It happens a lot on the job. The assistant instructor is alive, and is worried sick about you. I'm glad I can tell her you're fine."

"…If these are your honest feelings, I'm grateful."

"You've become wary." Houzen smiled bitterly. "'Tis encouraging, young miss. Me and all the disciples are looking forward to you returning and inheriting the clan."

"…I'm sorry." Rem bowed her head slightly. "I am Diablo's wife, when all is said and done."

Houzen turned his gaze to Diablo.

"A lot of the disciples thought badly of you when they heard some demon had put an 《Enslavement Collar》 on the young miss…"

Diablo replied with silence.

"But in the end, we're a mere clan of martial artists. We pay our respects to the strong, and a man who can beat the assistant instructor is certainly worthy. If anything, we would love for you to liven up the Gadou clan's future."

"…Mm."

Diablo was surprised they had said that.

"Oh," Houzen then appended, as if recalling something. "And the assistant instructor said to tell you she'll win next time."

"I see," Diablo shrugged.

The Gadou clan acknowledged the strong and always sought further battles. That was their way of life.

"…Let's stop talking about the future and focus on the present." Rem brought the conversation back on track. "Are we considered fugitives now?"

"You are. I don't recommend going into that inn town. There are a thousand soldiers lying in wait there."

"…Was the Gadou clan requested to help capture us?"

"No. All we got was a warning that they would stomp us out if we sided with you."

"…I see."

Rem was the previous clan head's daughter and the current head's niece. The kingdom probably feared that if they had the clan pursue her, they would betray the kingdom upon catching her. So they didn't ask them to join in the pursuit, but simply warned them not to get involved. A fair compromise, all things considered.

"...But if that's the case, why are you here?" Rem cocked her head.

"To side with you, of course."

"...I don't follow. Didn't they warn you to not get involved with me?"

"Well, that's why it's only me here." Houzen narrowed his eyes. "This carriage should have everything you need. Please, make use of it."

Rem's mouth fell open in shock.

"Won't you be in huge trouble if anyone finds out?!"

"Can we really say that we want you to come back if we stay on your side when everything's fine but turn on you when things get bad? We all want you to live and carry on the clan."

"...I'm not worth that much... Uncle and Auntie can have children too, can't they?"

"We'd be happy if they did, but they're both unmarried. And most of all, your skill exceeds even the previous head's."

"...I don't think that's true."

But arguing over that now would be counterproductive. Soldiers on patrol might spot them if they dawdled for too long.

"Whatever you choose to do is your path to carve out, and we will support it however we can," Houzen shrugged. "But for now, you have to prioritize your safety. Go straight for the kingdom of Greenwood and don't stop in any towns."

"...Thank you," Rem said, choosing to take the carriage he lent them.

It was a medium-sized carriage with a canopy, and its wagon was packed with preserved food. With this much, the three of them should be able to reach Greenwood no problem, assuming they didn't make any stops on their way. There was a bed in the wagon, too.

"I assumed you might need this." Houzen smiled.

"…I likely will, yes."

A medium-sized carriage would likely shake quite a bit, kicking up Rem's motion sickness. Rem climbed up to the coachman's seat and grabbed hold of the reins.

"Houzen… I'm very grateful to you. But I don't think I'll be able to live up to your expectations."

"Us disciples are just doing what we want."

"…Out of obligation for my father?"

Houzen's expression became oddly feline-like.

"No…" he replied, his cat ears twitching. "We haven't forgotten our debt to the previous head of the clan, but… All of us disciples are, without exception, in love with you, young miss."

"…Huh?!"

"Now, go on. And take care!"

The horse was seemingly well-trained, as it took off with that verbal cue from Houzen, pulling the carriage along.

†

Rem stayed silent until Houzen was out of sight, and then snuck a glance at Diablo.

"…Diablo? He… just confessed to me."

"Huh? Ah, yes, so it seems."

"…You always keep acting like what people are talking about has nothing to do with you."

"Th-That's not true."

"Then say something." Rem said, and as a blush came over her cheeks added, "as my… h-husband."

Diablo felt his own face go red.

"A-Ah… You belong to me. I won't relinquish you to some lowly disciple."

"Heheh…"

Rem's thin tail wagged from side to side, and she leaned her shoulder against his.

"…That's right. I belong to the Demon Lord Diablo."

Diablo stiffened despite himself, feeling the sensation of her shoulder just barely touching him.

Omnomnomnom…

Meanwhile, Shera was stuffing her cheeks back in the wagon, eating the preserved food.

"Yummy!"

"…Are you sure you're not eating too much?"

"You want some too, Rem? It's really good! Really!"

"…I'll eat a bit, I guess."

Shera then extended a sausage toward them.

"Here, Diablo. Say 'aaah'."

Rem's eyes widened.

"Th-That's cheap, Shera! I prepared that sausage!"

"Rem, forward, keep your eyes on the road!"

"Aaaaah?!"

Diablo found himself smirking wryly. They were in quite the huge mess, what with the Kingdom of Lyferia being after them, but this moment felt like a brief, peaceful moment of bliss.

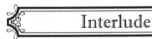

Interlude

The setting sun washed the eastern citadel city of Kenstone over with red. With the death of the garrisoned forces' commanding officer, the war hero Kudanis, the soldiers all lost their motivation to fight. The Gelmed Empire's Magimatic Sols were simply too powerful…

And now there were six of them. The Lyferian army surrendered, and Kenstone was occupied by the Empire. The soldiers and civilians were gathered in the eastern square where the Magimatic Sols stood. The unit's captain was Aira, a Kobold with a fox's ears and tail. The other pilots were also girls from races that fell into the therianthrope category.

A violet-colored Magimatic Sol opened, and from it descended a girl with long, equally violet hair that extended down to her legs. She had pointed horns atop her head — an Oni girl. A maid hurried to meet her as she disembarked, handing her a uniform. Upon exiting a Magimatic Sol, the girls were essentially naked.

She put on the uniform and scooped up her hair. Upon noticing someone was approaching her, her stern expression melted into a pleasant smile.

"Good work out there, Aira!" she said.

"Hey, Migurtha. Right back at you."

The Oni girl piloting the violet Magimatic Sol was Corporal Migurtha. The one who approached her was a female Kobold, Captain Aira. The two were of different races and different ranks, but they were the best of friends. While they couldn't afford to do so in more formal situations, most of the time they treated each other with no reservations.

"I'm sorry, Aira. I was late to regroup…"

"No, if anything, I'm surprised you made it before sundown. Good work, Migurtha."

"I had to make it before the main force, after all."

"To be honest… I think it'd be best if I were the only one who reported to him…"

"What are you saying? I can't let you do that."

"But this was my blunder."

"That's not true! This entire operation is messed up to begin with. They split our forces chasing the enemy's remnants and then expect you to launch an invasion?! And with Arjanos and its melee armaments, too!"

"Migurtha… That's enough…"

"They're coming."

Aira and Migurtha's expressions stiffened and they clicked their heels. Everyone else, who were on their breaks, ran over as well. Rikka and Erina's expressions were strained with stress. The sound of heavy cavalry approaching reached their ears. And…

Walking at the cavalry's back, accompanied by his subordinates, was a fat, round-bellied Human man. He was a middle-aged man, and his eyes were covered by a metal plate. Aira and the other girls were clad in black uniforms, but his was white and adorned with golden ornaments. His name was Doriadanph: a magimatic mage of the Gelmed Empire and the commander of the invasion forces. He stopped in front of the girls.

"Hmph. So the capture of the citadel city went… according to schedule, I see."

"Yes, sir!" Aira replied.

"However… Unless my eyes are playing tricks on me, there are only six Magimatic Sols here. Where's 《Arjanos of the Silver》?"

"Its nerve center was damaged, so I had it stored in the dimensional interstice."

"…Damaged?" Doriadanph clenched his teeth. "Perhaps my age is catching up with me and my hearing isn't what it used to be, but… Did you just say it was damaged?"

"It was damaged because of me. My apologies."

"Oh? So you're saying… You lost a Magimatic Sol to Lyferian soldiers with their primitive iron spears and wooden arrows?"

"I did not lose it… No, my apologies!"

"Is that the posture one apologizes with?"

"Nng…"

Aira dropped to her knees. Erina made to open her mouth, but Migurtha silenced her with a raised hand. Rikka and the other soldiers all knew already that Lyferia wasn't as weak as Doriadanph made it out to be. Still, Aira lowered her head.

"I apologize for damaging the precious unit bequeathed to me by His Imperial Majesty the Emperor!"

"I said lower… your… head!" Doriadanph stepped on the back of her head.

He pressed his weight on her, pushing Aira's face into the ground with a thump.

"Guh?!"

"Have you forgotten His Imperial Majesty's kindness, you ungrateful cur?! Remind me, why is it that you therianthropes are welcomed in the sacred territories of the Empire?!"

"B-Because of… His Imperial Majesty's… benevolent heart…!"

"Then why? Why do you disappoint His Imperial Majesty?!"

"M-My apolo…"

"You filthy beasts! There are plenty waiting in line to fill your roles!"

He put more weight onto his foot to hurt Aira further. A crunching sound rang out from beneath her head.

"Guh?! Aaah?!"

"You're not thinking of rebelling… Are you?!"

"I-I would… never…!"

Red fluid spread out on the ground. Blood was leaking out of Aira's broken nose. Erina held her breath anxiously, but noticed that Migurtha's hand, which blocked her path forward, was shaking.

"Kh…" She grit her teeth.

"Ah… Captain Aira, remind me, what was your village called again?"

"Please! Don't harm the village!"

"Oh ho… But without a Magimatic Sol, you're nothing more than a stinking animal." He grinded his heel over Aira's head.

"Ugh…"

But then Doriadanph seemed to recall something.

"Oh, come to think of it… We do have one Magimatic Sol without a pilot."

"Ah?!"

"Try piloting 《Goldinus of the Gold》."

A shiver ran through Aira's shoulders, and before Erina could say anything, Migurtha cried out.

"Please, wait!"

Doriadanph swung around, punching Migurtha straight in the face.

"Just who… gave you permission to speak?"

"…My apologies," Migurtha said, blood trickling from her lip. "But Goldinus… hasn't had any compatible pilots yet… It consumed all of its test subjects."

"Perhaps she'll be compatible."

"Please, reconsider. If we lose Captain Aira, it will be difficult to continue our invasion according to plan."

"…You dare share your opinion with me… you filthy little imp…?"

"Pardon my impudence! The six of us will endeavor to make up for Arjanos' share of the work! But please, do reconsider! Captain Aira is a skilled commander, she's precious manpower we cannot afford to lose!"

Doriadanph dropped his gaze to his feet and finally moved away his foot.

"Very well. I will leave the captain to her role, as is."

"Thank you very much!" Migurtha bowed her head.

"However… You *will* take responsibility for speaking out of turn, Corporal. I sentence you to… a hundred whippings."

The others made to argue, but Migurtha responded before anyone else could else could speak.

"I humbly accept my punishment!"

Doriadanph scoffed at her and turned his back.

"…Call the magimatic engineers," he told his attendant. "Have Arjanos of the Silver repaired."

"Yes, sir!" The attendant saluted and was about to run off, only to be stopped once more by Doriadanph.

"Wait. Have the seekers leave their holes, too… We still need to sniff her out."

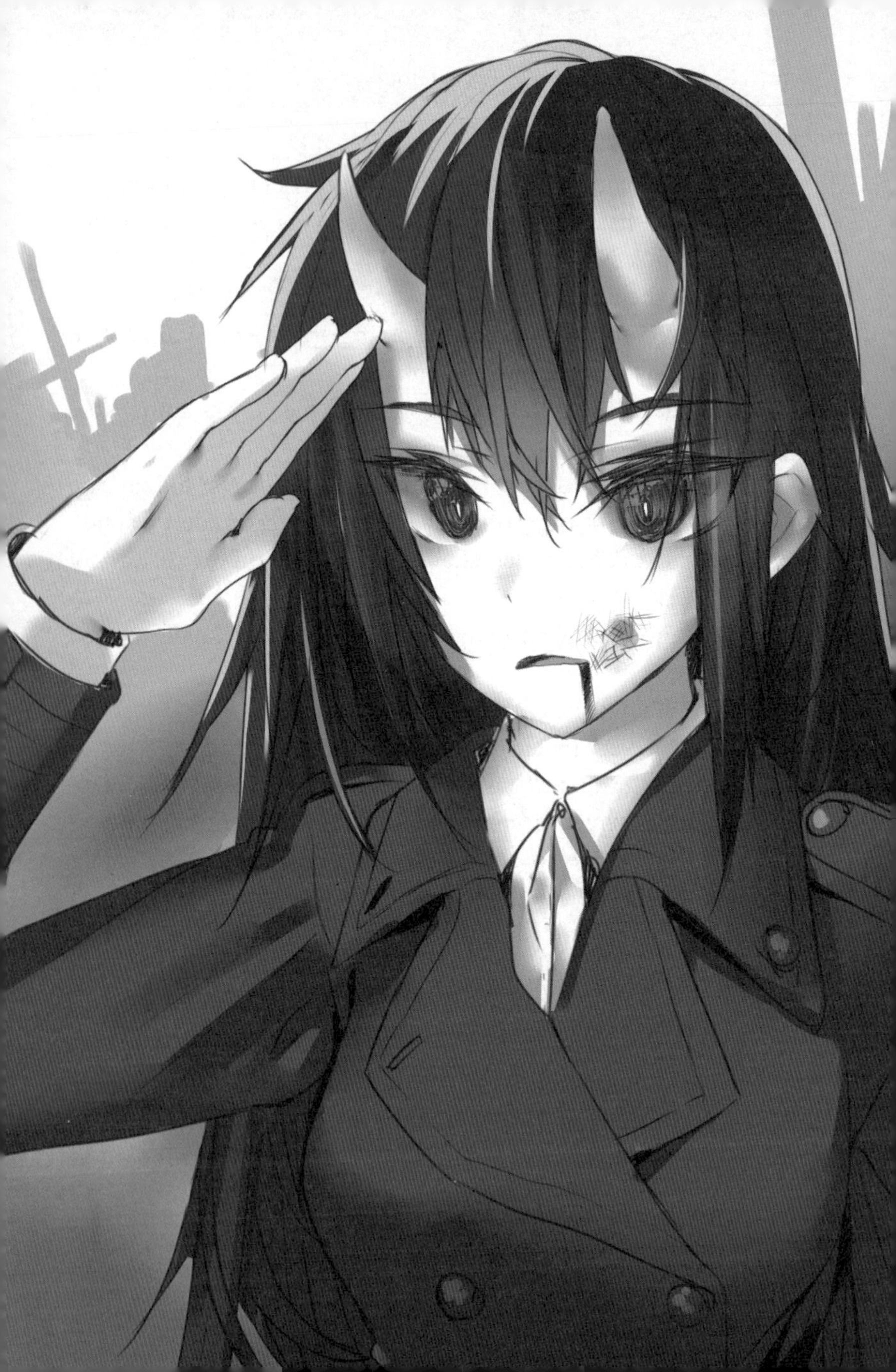

†

With their commander gone, the girls gathered around Aira and helped her to her feet.

"Lady Aira, your nose…" Erina said with tears in her eyes.

Blood dripped from it freely, forming dark red stains on her black uniform.

"Yes, looks like I broke my nose… I'll be fine. This will heal up in no time."

"Let me!" Rikka, a dryad, extended her hands forward. A white flash enveloped Aira and the bleeding suddenly stopped.

"I'm sure you're tired too, Rikka, but I…"

"I'm completely, totally fine!"

Aira then turned her gaze to Migurtha.

"I'm sorry."

"Don't let it bother you. This is a hundred times better than letting that crazy magimatic mage make you into his toy."

"Goldinus of the Gold… They say it's the strongest Magimatic Sol…"

"That's nonsense! That thing is just an execution chamber!"

"Right… Thank you. You saved me."

Aira bowed to her and then looked around at her companions.

"Whoaaa…"

Erina, who had hair a shade of angrier red, wept bitter tears. She was naturally very short, so she looked like a sobbing child.

"Grr… Lady Aira…"

The pilot of the grey Magimatic Sol was Bakki, who was currently visibly enraged. She had kept her composure this time, but was the quickest to anger of them all. She was a werewolf.

"Dammit!" She slammed her right fist into her left fist. "If only they didn't have everyone back home at the village as hostages!"

Another in the group was Saya, who had emerald green hair. She was a nekomata, and the youngest of the group, making her effectively a kitten. She was always silent and expressionless, and her comrades couldn't tell what she was thinking… But right now it was clear she was sad. Her triangular ears flattened against her head and her eyes were moist with tears.

Toaha, a yellow Lamia, disembarked her Magimatic Sol. She was very much their group's ace, but it was as if half of her heart remained within the unit. Rumor had it that her compatibility with her Magimatic Sol was too high. Even in this situation, she could only smile faintly.

"It's a good thing you're still alive, Aira," she said blankly. "We can eat together again."

"…Right."

Chapter 2 ※ Trying to be a Paladin Captain

There were checkpoints along the road. It seemed they were wary of letting criminals approach the capital, and they collected taxes based on cargo and how many people were traveling. Naturally, the checkpoints were built in positions that made it difficult to get around them.

Diablo stopped the carriage at the road's shoulder and spread out a map in the wagon.

"What should we do?" Rem said pensively. "We don't have to go through here if we go straight to Greenwood."

The map Houzen provided them detailed a path that didn't go through any checkpoints, but it headed away from the capital.

"But Sylvie and Horn are still in the capital, right?" Shera leaned forward.

"...There's a chance they've already been apprehended."

The king and his lackeys already knew Sylvie and Horn had ties with Diablo. It was hard to imagine nothing had happened to them while they stayed in the heart of Kingdom territory.

"Sylvie and Horn are both clever and quick on their feet. I'm sure they're fine."

"...I doubt that's the problem, but... Still, I can't see Sylvie getting caught without some plan."

"Yep, yep!"

"...However, they probably aren't waiting idly in the hotel we decided on. How do we get in touch with them?"

"Maybe we could write Lumachina or Alicia a letter?"

"...All letters get inspected at the checkpoints. I doubt any we send will reach their destination."

"Then let's have my 《Turkey Shot》 deliver it! It can fly!"

"...You underestimate the capital's aerial defenders. Even wyverns can't approach it."

"Then maybe it can swim in?"

"...They have guards set up at the water canals, too."

"But the capital's so big!"

"...Yes, the capital is quite large. It's ten times Faltra's size. We can't infiltrate the castle at the center, but if it's just going into the city, it might be possible."

"We'll work something out when we get there!"

"...You make it sound easier than it is."

Diablo pondered over the matter while not taking part in the conversation. Their current quest was to regroup with Sylvie and Horn and then escape the capital. Escaping wouldn't be a problem, though, since teleportation allowed for up to six people. They'd be able to get back to Faltra in the blink of an eye.

He didn't tell Houzen this since he'd gone through the trouble of preparing a carriage, but the three of them could simply teleport to Greenwood if that was what they wanted to do. That magic did exist in this world, though its use wasn't widespread.

The problem here is regrouping with Horn and Sylvie.

After considering multiple possible scenarios, Diablo decided on a plan.

"Alright," he said.

"...Did you think of something?" Rem asked.

"What, what?!" Shera looked at him with glittering eyes.

Diablo reached for his pouch.

"Annihilation."

"…I see."

"Huh?! You can't do that!"

"Hmph." Diablo shrugged.

It was a joke. Rem saw through it and ignored him entirely.

"Geez, you startled me." Shera, though, was a bit naive.

"…So, what's your real plan?" Rem asked him with a chilly voice.

"Passing through the checkpoint with our carriage wouldn't be possible." He crossed his arms. "So we'll use a nearby church. Churches are said to be independent of royal law. A letter might be too much, but we can ask the priests to pass a message to Lumachina."

"Alright, let's do that!" Shera gave a big nod.

Rem seemed to think things through a bit longer, but eventually shrugged.

"…I agree. But I'd like to contribute a bit to this plan, if you don't mind."

Diablo always worked alone, so the idea of 'deciding on what to do together' was a bit foreign to him. Apologizing felt wrong, so he simply didn't react. Rem moved the topic forward, though, not letting go of the conversation.

"…That said… Will the church cooperate with us? How do we know they won't sell us out to the king?"

"No, a priest wouldn't do that!"

"…I think we've seen plenty of priests that act only in their self-interest."

True, that was a risk. But Diablo wasn't one to rely on faith without any plan in mind.

"We use this."

Diablo pulled a silver holy mark from his pouch — the Paladin Captain's mark.

"What's that?" Shera asked, tilting her head quizzically.

"You don't know? Hmm, come to think of it, you were bedridden when I got this."

"…It's my first time seeing it too, but is that holy mark a Paladin Captain's mark?"

"Mm." Diablo nodded.

"Paladin Captain?" Shera still seemed confused.

"…Lumachina used her authority as High Priest to place Diablo in the position of Paladin Captain."

"Huh?! That's amazing!"

Saying he was placed in that position was a bit faulty. He was only given, and had accepted, this holy mark. He'd done nothing in the capacity of a Paladin Captain, and Lumachina didn't expect him to do anything of the sort either.

"But it makes sense." Shera nodded, seemingly convinced. "Diablo did save the church, after all."

"Hmph… I have never once tried to save anyone."

Diablo and his group had helped reform the church by driving out a corrupt group called the Cardinal Authority. In doing so, they'd saved not only the church, but Lyferia as a whole. But since that wasn't the Demon Lord-ly thing to do, Diablo scoffed and disregarded the idea.

Lumachina gave him this mark as the greatest form of gratitude she could offer. If he identifies himself as a Paladin Captain, he would be welcomed at any church. The people there would cooperate with him to the best of their abilities… Or so she had said. He had never used it before, since a Demon Lord calling himself a Paladin Captain was all sorts of strange.

"…If we were to visit the church while wanted, the priests would surrender us to the army." Rem nodded. "But if we're with a Paladin Captain, everything changes. The pawns of the church betraying a higher-up could cause a great scandal."

"Mm."

"…The church has its own religious jurisdiction. Even if we're criminals, only the High Priest would have the authority to judge us."

That was the logic behind it, at least. Diablo was attacked by an odd sense of unease, but he said nothing.

"Let's head to the nearby town," Rem said, moving the carriage. "There's a fairly large church there."

The horse's hooves clicked against the road.

"Go, go♪" Shera pumped her fist into the air.

"…With a clip clop."

"Go, go♪"

†

The following morning…

Kenstone approached the second day of its occupation. Having received an ominous report, Aira took off toward the western square. Armed imperial soldiers stood around the square, menacing the Lyferian civilians. The townsfolk were unarmed, so this didn't count as combat. If they did clash, it would result in a one-sided massacre.

Aira looked away, her gaze falling on a group of civilians being loaded onto carts. She ran toward it.

"Wait!"

"My, if it isn't the good captain."

The one in command of this place was a man in black clothing, his mouth covered with a mask that resembled a raven's beak. He was a seeker, likely brought over by Doriadanph.

"What are you doing?!"

"As you can see, I'm performing a manhunt."

Aira turned her gaze to the carriage. It was full of demis of many different races and ages, all of them with black hair, and likely all of them female. There were Pantherians, Dwarves, and Grasswalkers, but no Humans or Elves.

"I've heard nothing of this."

"I see. So you weren't told." The man's voice was muffled because of the beak.

"Please refrain from meddling needlessly with Lyferia's citizens," she said with a strong tone. "Maintaining public order in our occupied territories is *my* duty."

"This isn't needless meddling. I'm acting under the imperial decree of the emperor himself, according to the commander. You'd do well to not interfere."

"An imperial order?!"

The emperor of the Gelmed Empire was already in old age. He was bedridden and very rarely moved. Aira didn't think he had any reason to gather women at this point.

A manhunt…?

"I'm just obeying orders." The seeker shrugged his shoulders. "I hold my life quite dear to me, after all."

"Kuh…" Aira gritted her teeth.

The citizens of Kenstone directed looks of sheer hatred in her direction. It was her who had guaranteed the citizens and soldiers' safety should they surrender, after all. And now this. Men in odd clothing were carrying their friends off. Their displeasure was understandable, but still, an imperial order meant her hands were tied. She could only stand by.

A memory of the past surfaced in her mind... Once, she had lived in her village along with her fellow Kobolds. But then soldiers armed with magimatic technology charged into their village, killed many of their men, and captured the rest of the villagers.

Aira was appraised as having 'strong force of will' and was thrown into Arjanos of the Silver. She thought she was going to be devoured alive... but as luck would have it, she was found compatible, which brought her to her position at present.

"...Come to think of it, back then... Only the black-haired ones were carried off somewhere else. I was sure they were chosen as candidates for the Magimatic Sols, but..."

"The 《Girl of the Vessel》 wasn't among the Kobolds, after all," the seeker said, narrowing his eyes.

She couldn't see his mouth because of the beak, but he may have been smirking.

"...What? What's that?"

"I don't know? That's who we've been looking for this whole time... Though there's no telling if she really exists."

"You should have been ordered not to kill any black-haired girls, too."

"Yes, that's right."

She'd thought it was for some humane reason, but looking back, it was strange indeed. All the black-haired girls in Aira's village were rounded up and taken away, never to return. She'd thought they simply weren't compatible with the Magimatic Sols, but was there another reason?

Just who or what was the Girl of the Vessel? The Empire was definitely hiding something.

"We… the Empire of Gelmed are fighting this war using magimatic technology to rule the world… to rid it of war, right?" Aira asked.

"You think I can answer that question?"

"…No."

His position was the same as Aira's. His hometown was conquered by the Empire, forcing him to obey.

"I'm simply doing as the commander ordered and gathering all the therianthropes and beast-like black-haired girls here," the seeker said, shifting his gaze to the girls. "You're better off not getting involved with this. For both of our sakes."

"But that's…"

"Captain, you value your comrades and the people of your homeland over the citizens of another country, correct? I feel the same way."

"Ugh…"

The sight of the people of Kenstone raising their voices in anxiety and displeasure reminded Aira of her own past. But she couldn't oppose the Empire to help them.

†

According to the map, their destination was close, but they had to take the long way around due to a suspension bridge collapse. It took them several days to reach the town.

"…This should be the place."

"Rem, you look kinda pale."

"…I'm relatively better off when I'm in the driver's seat holding the reins."

Still, the road was bumpy enough to kick up her motion sickness. Diablo himself was pretty queasy from having his backside kicked up by all the jolting. He felt like he'd vomit immediately if his stomach was stimulated in any way. Shera was the only one to remain perky.

"Are you all right? Want some bacon?"

"…Talk to me about food later, please," Rem replied with a heavy voice.

Their carriage approached the town.

"It's not really a small town," Shera said, seemingly impressed.

"…Yes, it has about one hundred buildings."

"And a really big fence!"

"…That's to keep animals out. There are some guards at the gate, too. Only a couple of them, though."

"Will we be all right? Has word gotten out that Diablo is wanted?"

"…We can't know for sure, but I think we're still in the clear," Rem nodded.

"Really?"

Letters were the prime method of communication in this world. Some important cities and fortresses seemed to have some magical means of communication, but for the most part, it was letters. Plus, there was no printing press, to say nothing of copy machines.

"…If they wanted to distribute wanted posters that included our personal descriptions, they'd have to copy them by hand."

"Oooh, right. That sounds hard."

"…Which is why the information doesn't circulate as fast to places that aren't as important. Like this town, a ways off the highway."

"Yeah, I don't think they'd send anything here!"

"…There's no way of knowing for sure, though."

"Uuu… God, pretty please! I wanna sleep in a warm bed for once."

A pragmatic wish, if there ever was one.

Their carriage rolled down the road, and two guards apprehensively approached to inspect the unfamiliar vehicle. But when they looked at the driver's seat, they suddenly blushed.

"Whoa, they're gorgeous…!"

"H-Hey, cut it out! Wait up. Who are you people?"

The Human gatekeepers were seemingly taken aback by Rem and Shera's beauty. Very few actually fell in love with those of other races, but standards of beauty were another matter, and Rem and Shera were attractive enough that people turned to look at them in the streets.

And girls that pretty were with some Demon man who had put 《Enslavement Collars》 on them… This could spell trouble.

"Who are we, you ask…?" Diablo glared at the guards. "To think you backwater hicks have not heard of me… Etch my name into your heart as you take shame in your ignorance! For it is Diablo, a—"

"Aaah, aaaah!" Shera waved her hands.

"He's a… very important person from the church!" Rem leaned forward, her tail swinging nervously. "Would you be so kind as to point us in the direction of this town's church?!"

Her voice was uncharacteristically high-pitched and her wagging tail was positively slapping the 'very important person' in question across the face, but… he was just about to identify himself as a Demon Lord, as he typically did.

Right, I'm supposed to be pretending to be a Paladin Captain now…

In terms of acting, it didn't matter if he was pretending to be a Demon Lord or a Paladin Captain. So long as he wasn't speaking with his own voice, the words would come out. Diablo produced the silver holy mark.

"I am a Paladin Captain. Let me see this town's priest."

The flustered guards stiffened as if they'd been hit by petrification magic.

"P-P-P-Paladin Captain?!" "A Paladin Captain?!"

"...Which way to the town's church?" Rem asked again.

"W-We'll escort you there!"

The two ran into the town. Was it really okay for the gate guards to be gone, though?

Well, this is the sticks, so it's probably calm around here...

"Thank goodness...!" Shera sighed in relief.

She was right. It seemed the town hadn't gotten word about Diablo yet.

†

Rem said it was a fairly large church, but if Diablo had to describe it, it wasn't so much a large place as it was a building with a lot of history behind it.

Or, put another way, it was just old.

Pillars made of wood supported walls made of mud, and its roof was made of earth, too. It was an unusual building by Lyferia's standards.

"...I don't think this kind of architecture was in use even a hundred years ago. It must be older than that... Or it was intentionally built in an archaic style."

A female Dwarf clad in a priest's garb exited the building.

"This church was built in this spot 300 years ago. Saint Clasa built it here to save the people of this land."

She had the Dwarven characteristics Diablo was used to — she was short with a plump chest, as well as dog ears and a tail. In her case, she had the lopped ears of a labrador.

"Welcome to the old church of Towa!"

"E-Erm!" The gatekeepers made to say something, but she simply nodded kindly and cut them off.

"These people are fine. Return to your duties."

"Ah… Yes, understood!" The two bowed their heads and left for the gates.

"…Do you know about us?" Rem asked.

Rem was usually calm, but her tone was especially level. She was likely quite cautious.

"No, I don't." The Dwarf priest cocked her head. "But during my morning prayers, I'd heard that important guests should be arriving today…"

"…A divine revelation?"

"Oh, it's nothing so grand. Only the High Priest can hear God's voice. You could call it hearsay."

"Hearsay?" Shera tilted her head quizzically.

The word normally implied unreliable rumors, but…

"Come in." She gestured for them to enter the church. "I haven't much to welcome you, but I can serve you some hot milk."

"Yay!" Shera followed her without a hint of caution.

What she said seemed a bit suspect, but they had nothing to prove it was. Diablo followed Rem inside. The interior of the earthen church wasn't what they were used to. It felt more like they were in a basement than inside a building. Wooden pillars supported the dirt that made up the ceiling, and around them chairs were set up.

There were no windows for illumination, and so candles lit up the place even during the day.

"Sit wherever you'd like," the Dwarven priest said before going through a door in the back of the room. A few moments later, she returned carrying a tray lined with wooden cups full of hot milk.

"Wow, thank you!"

"…Thank you very much."

Shera and Rem accepted the cups.

"Here you are." The priest handed Diablo a cup. "It's goat milk."

"Mm."

The word 'milk' tempted Diablo to sneak a peek at the priest's bosom, but he consciously fixed his gaze on his hands. He was supposed to be a Paladin Captain right now. Ogling a woman's breasts would just make his acting all the more unconvincing.

"…Are you the only priest here?" Rem asked, looking around curiously.

The Dwarven priest nodded, placing a hand over her considerable chest. She introduced herself with a kind voice.

"Yes. I am called Rilitana."

"…I'm Rem Galleu, and this is Shera. We're both adventurers. And this man right here is…"

Diablo held up the silver holy mark.

"That's a Paladin Captain's…?!" Rilitana's eyes widened.

"Mmm."

"I never imagined you'd visit a small town like ours… My apologies."

She bowed down on the wooden floor and brought her hands together. Diablo felt an uncomfortable itch run down his spine. When he acted as a Demon Lord, he only ever saw challengers with weapons in hand and enmity in their eyes. He would only provoke them and stayed focused on battle.

But being a Paladin Captain was different. People respected him, and he was required to behave like a decent person.

Can I do that? Can I speak like a mature person in this position?

He was getting nervous. Thankfully, Rem took over the negotiations.

"…We have turned against the king, due to certain circumstances. We don't intend to cause any trouble, but we need to get in contact with our comrades in the capital."

"Huh?! You turned against His Majesty?!"

"…We want you to deliver a message to the High Priest Lumachina."

A letter would be inspected at the checkpoints, so they needed a priest who would go to the Grand Cathedral for them.

Diablo opened his mouth, preparing to make a request.

You are a Paladin Captain. A Paladin Captain. A Paladin Captain…

"Rejoice, for you can be of use to the Demon Lord Diablo!"

But old habits die way, way too hard.

"D-Demon Lord…?" Rilitana stiffened.

Gaaaaaaaaaaaaaah! Wait, no, gimme a redo! Another try! Another try! C'mon, just give me a redo!

He'd been acting out the part of a Demon Lord for so long, it slipped out naturally. A waterfall of sweat ran down Diablo's back. He'd screwed it all up. Rem and Shera were panicking, too.

"N-No, that's not what he meant!"

"Yeah, he meant, uhm!"

But they couldn't come up with anything else.

"You're just as I've heard…" Rilitana eyed Diablo closely. "You really are the Paladin Captain."

"Aah?!" He screeched in an utterly pathetic voice.

"The High Priest had once told me," Rilitana said. "The current Paladin Captain is a man who 'is an adventurer playing the part of a Demon Lord, but is actually God's incarnation.'"

Isn't she laying it a little too thick with that backstory…?

Lumachina did say she'd explained his 'circumstances' to the believers, but she made him out to be one real idiot.

I'm actually a shut-in gamer from another world, though.

Diablo couldn't exactly say that, so he simply fixed his sitting posture.

"Hmph… I have told Lumachina time and again that I am not God."

"Heheh… Yes, she said that, too."

"Haaaaa~" Shera sighed with relief. "Thank goodness you believe us…"

"…The High Priest has the highest authority in the church," Rem said. "She's not someone a regional priest can just speak to casually. Who are you, really?"

"I really am just a regular priest. Except… When the current High Priest was but a girl, her parents brought her to this land while on a pilgrimage."

Diablo jolted up upon hearing the word 'pilgrimage'. To him, it described visiting sites that were used as inspiration for scenes in anime. Rilitana was talking about the more traditional sense of the word, though — a journey where one visited religious sites.

"I could sense Lady Lumachina was close to the Lord, and took her to the Grand Cathedral," Rilitana said nostalgically.

"…You did that?!"

"Her sublime grandness was clear to all."

Really? Diablo wondered.

When Diablo first met Lumachina, she was attacked by the Paladin Gewalt's summon beast and was stark naked, since it had torn off her clothes. He felt himself blushing at the memory. It was sublime, but in a much different sort of way.

"When Lumachina... I mean, when Her Eminence prays, it does indeed feel like she can reach the heavens."

"Yep, yep!" Shera agreed. "The light goes woooooosh all the way up to the sky!"

"It was because Lady Lumachina could hear the voice of God that she was made the High Priest." Rilitana brought her hands together. "But the title has brought great trouble and pain on her. And the one who saved her... was the current Paladin Captain. I cannot overstate my gratitude."

"Mm." Diablo crossed his arms and nodded.

He tried to not say any more needless things.

"I'm rather well known at the checkpoints leading up to the capital from here." Rilitana proposed, "if I go along with you, you should be able to reach the Grand Cathedral in the capital even with the king's order in effect. What do you say?"

"Wow, that sounds great!" Shera brought her hands together.

True, it was more reliable than entrusting her with a message, and it would allow them to get into the capital. And once they regrouped, he could just teleport them out.

"...If that's true, it would be quite helpful," Rem said cautiously. "Will the soldiers at the checkpoints really listen to you, though?"

"They look up to the priests of their regions."

"...I imagine they do."

"The local church is important for everyday life, after all."

Making light of the church didn't just make life harder for someone. At worst, the believers could even make an attempt on such a person's life.

"...But since you're the person who discovered the High Priest, they'll treat you differently. It wouldn't be odd for you to be part of the Cardinal Authority."

Could they really trust her, though? Even if she didn't have any malicious intent, there was no guarantee the priests in the towns beyond the checkpoints would listen to her. And the guards might not let suspicious people through regardless of what a priest had to say.

However, they didn't have any other way.

"I allow it, Rilitana. Guide us to the capital."

"I promise that I will, Sir Paladin Captain!"

†

They needed to have their carriage's horse rest, and the town's lone priest couldn't leave for long without letting the people know. The church supported the town's day-to-day activities, after all. And so Rilitana told the mayor she'd be gone for a time, leaving out the details.

Also, with the church being as old as it is, Rilitana needed to make sure someone looked after the building in her absence. She also sent messengers to her friends in the neighboring towns, making sure priests would show up periodically.

And so, a whole day passed by.

The following day, they were preparing to leave. Diablo stood in front of the dresser with a sour expression.

"Is this… really necessary?"

"I might be a priest, but we're bound to run into troops that take their jobs too seriously," Rilitana nodded gravely. "It's important we don't look suspicious."

"That much goes without saying."

"Fix that tone, please!"

"Guh…"

Diablo had a long-haired wig on his head.

"About your name, I figured we could go with Diala. What do you think?"

"Kuh…"

The tattoos that marked him as a Demon were hidden behind makeup, and he wore a comfortable dress. To any onlooker, Diablo — or rather, Diala — looked like a normal Human female.

Is she telling a Demon Lord like me to humiliate myself in public?!

He could only seethe internally. But Rilitana said "A Paladin Captain should prioritize their ambition over their appearance" with eyes full of faith, so he couldn't decline.

And it was true that if crossdressing would save him trouble and get him to the capital that much faster, it was worth it. He couldn't help but wonder what Sylvie and Horn were going through in the capital right now…

But Diablo and his group had to worry for their own safety, too. It wasn't just Diablo in trouble here, but Rem and Shera as well. If they could avoid fighting altogether, it would be for the best.

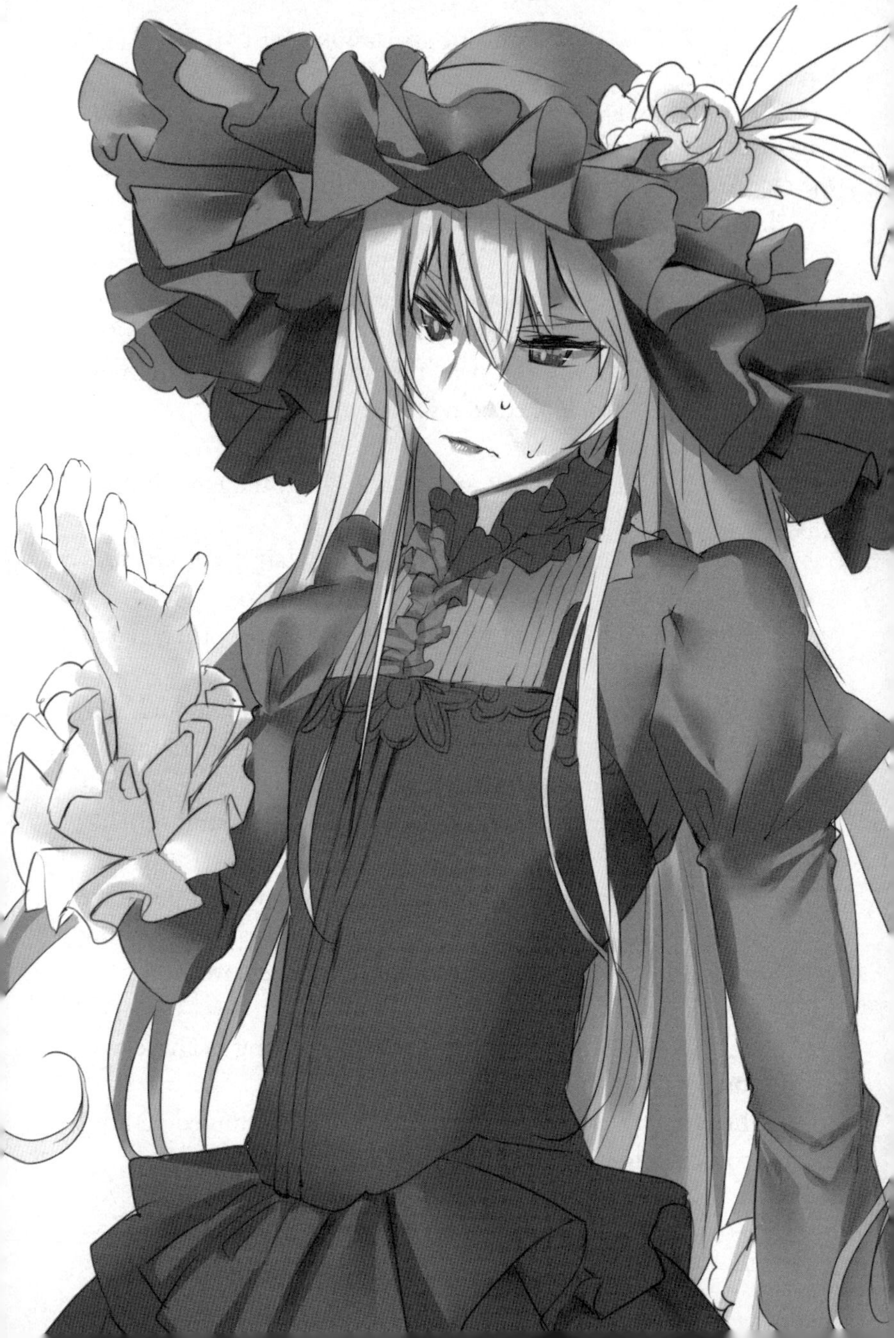

The room's door swung open and two young men walked in. One of them was a young Pantherian with the orange hair typical of the race. He eyed Diablo... Diala, with sparkling eyes.

"...Diablo, you look lovely! Like a real noble lady."

"Yep! You're really pretty!" The Elf boy nodded.

Those two 'boys' were actually Rem and Shera, who were crossdressing as men. Rem's characteristic black hair was stuffed under a short-haired wig that was the bright shade of hair most Pantherians had. Shera looked convincing, too.

"A real metamorphosis."

"Heheh... It's a little tight around the chest, though..." Shera giggled.

Shera's own unique characteristic, her large bosom, was completely gone, too.

"...Meanwhile, I just had to put these clothes on." Rem glared at her.

To the onlookers, the three of them together would look like a slightly bulky noble lady and two demi boys... or not. Thanks to the Enslavement Collars clasped around the so-called boys' necks, it looked more like a slightly crazy noble lady walking around with her two slave boys.

"We do have a carriage..." Rilitana said pensively. "I guess we could say you're a spoiled noble's daughter on her way to an evening party in the capital, and we've been assigned to watch over you."

"...That's awfully specific."

"Yes, well... When you've been a priest for as long as I have, you see all sorts of things."

Rilitana's gaze turned distant, as if she were recalling something. Diablo chose not to pry and simply sighed.

"Enough. The details matter little. We must reach the capital as soon as possible, so I shan't ask you for the particularities of how we get there. But let us make haste!"

"Yes, let's leave right now, then."

Rilitana picked up her luggage and Shera hopped happily.

"Go, go~♪"

"...I like you better without those things blocking the view from your side. You should stay this way."

"Huh?! But it's so tight!"

Even when they looked like boys, the two of them were the same as always.

†

One week later...

Diablo's group had passed three checkpoints without incident. The time was noon, and the weather was clear. The sun shone above them, and it was warm enough to start sweating under the sunlight. It wasn't quite like Faltra, but the area was relatively warm. They were half a day away from the capital, and there was nothing left in their way. They'd likely be there by sunset.

"...Rilitana really is a wonderful priest," Rem said, seemingly in a good mood. "The very ideal of what a priest should be, even."

"Oh, that's not true," Rilitana said, covering her mouth modestly.

"But you're amazing!" Shera joined in on the praise. "You always sing so well when it's time for prayer, and your cooking is great, too!"

"I'm glad you enjoyed it."

Diablo thought she was like a mom. She really was skilled. They didn't have to fight anyone on the way here, so he didn't know how good of a healer she was, but... The melody of her prayers felt like they must even match Lumachina's. Perhaps that was only natural, since she did help Lumachina on her first steps to priesthood when she was young.

Rilitana didn't flinch away when she was surrounded by troops and spoke to the people in charge of the checkpoints clearly. She said she was 'well known', but she wasn't just talking about the priests in the areas of the checkpoints — she was looked up to as a teacher by many. Whenever the people ran into problems they couldn't solve, they came to her for help.

She was very much admired like a holy mother.

"...I really did mean what I said," Rem said. "Someone like you should have been chosen for the Cardinal Authority."

Rilitana cast down her gaze.

"I appreciate the sentiment, but I... I'm a Dwarf."

"Oh... I see. The Grand Cathedral is in the capital, and there's a great deal of discrimination around there."

"Weren't the members of the Cardinal Authority all Humans back when Vishos was in charge?" Diablo recalled.

"Yes," Rilitana affirmed. "It's not just that. Had Lady Lumachina not been a Human... She wouldn't have been appointed High Priest, even with all her talent."

"How foolish," Diablo said.

"...It really is," Rem agreed, baring her fangs.

"That's awful!" Even Shera, who was slow to anger, was annoyed.

"Who to believe, what to believe in, and what world you want are all different for each of us," Rilitana soothed them. "Good and evil are different from one's likes and dislikes... And there's not much to be done about that, sadly."

"...Still, racial discrimination shouldn't be tolerated."

"It might be wrong, but the fact remains that some people in the capital maintain those prejudices. If my being at Lady Lumachina's side would bring her trouble, then it would be for the best if I were not."

Diablo could imagine trouble stirring up over that. Vishos' Cardinal Authority were all slaughtered by the Order of Palace Knights. Apparently they'd had connections to the royal court, so the ringleader silenced them.

Lumachina did elect a new Cardinal Authority and invited Rilitana to join, but apparently she declined. Her town, as well as the matter of her race, kept her from accepting.

"That's kind of sad…" Shera said forlornly.

"It's fine." Rilitana shook her head. "If anything's the problem, it's that the suffocating lifestyle of the capital doesn't agree with me. I didn't refuse just because of the old church or my being a Dwarf. I had my own reasons."

Her cheeks suddenly flushed red.

"…Your own reasons?" Rem cocked her head curiously.

"I'm no good… I can't restrain myself." Rilitana looked outside the canopy.

Her gaze wasn't the same calm look she often had, but had a certain hunger to it.

"Is there something you wish for? Do not hide it, and be frank with it."

"…He's right, Rilitana," Rem said. "You shouldn't need to feel bashful around us."

"H-Huh? Can I really…?"

"What, what?" Shera leaned forward. "Do you want something? Anything you want to do?"

"Erm… I suppose it's something I'd like to do…"

"Then why not?"

Shera was as easygoing as ever and didn't ask for details.

"…Should we stop the carriage?" Rem wondered.

"No, there's no need to do that."

"…Then all the more so, don't feel reserved."

"Y-Yes."

Rilitana snuck a look in Diablo's direction. Her eyes were wavering.

"What is it?"

"No, it's just that… Uhm… This might be an unpleasant sight."

"Hmph… I am a Demon Lord. No matter what you do, it won't faze me."

"Thank you very much!" She gave a somehow-liberated smile. "Then, please excuse me…"

Rilitana reached for her priest's garb. Rem and Shera's eyes widened, and Diablo was struck speechless. Rilitana swiftly threw off her clothes.

"I just can't stand wearing thick clothes when it's this hot outside…!"

Yeah, I think I can see why she can't live in the city now! Diablo thought to himself.

Apparently she didn't put any underwear on to begin with, meaning she was now stark naked. She was a hard worker, so her features was toned, but perhaps because of her Dwarven physique, her bosom sagged a bit. Thick beads of sweat rolled down her skin.

Why did you take off ALL your clothes?! he nearly shouted, but apparently that was her wish. Diablo didn't like seeing other people's… peculiarities denied, nor was he one to deny them himself, so he didn't intend to judge her for it. Still, he didn't know where to look.

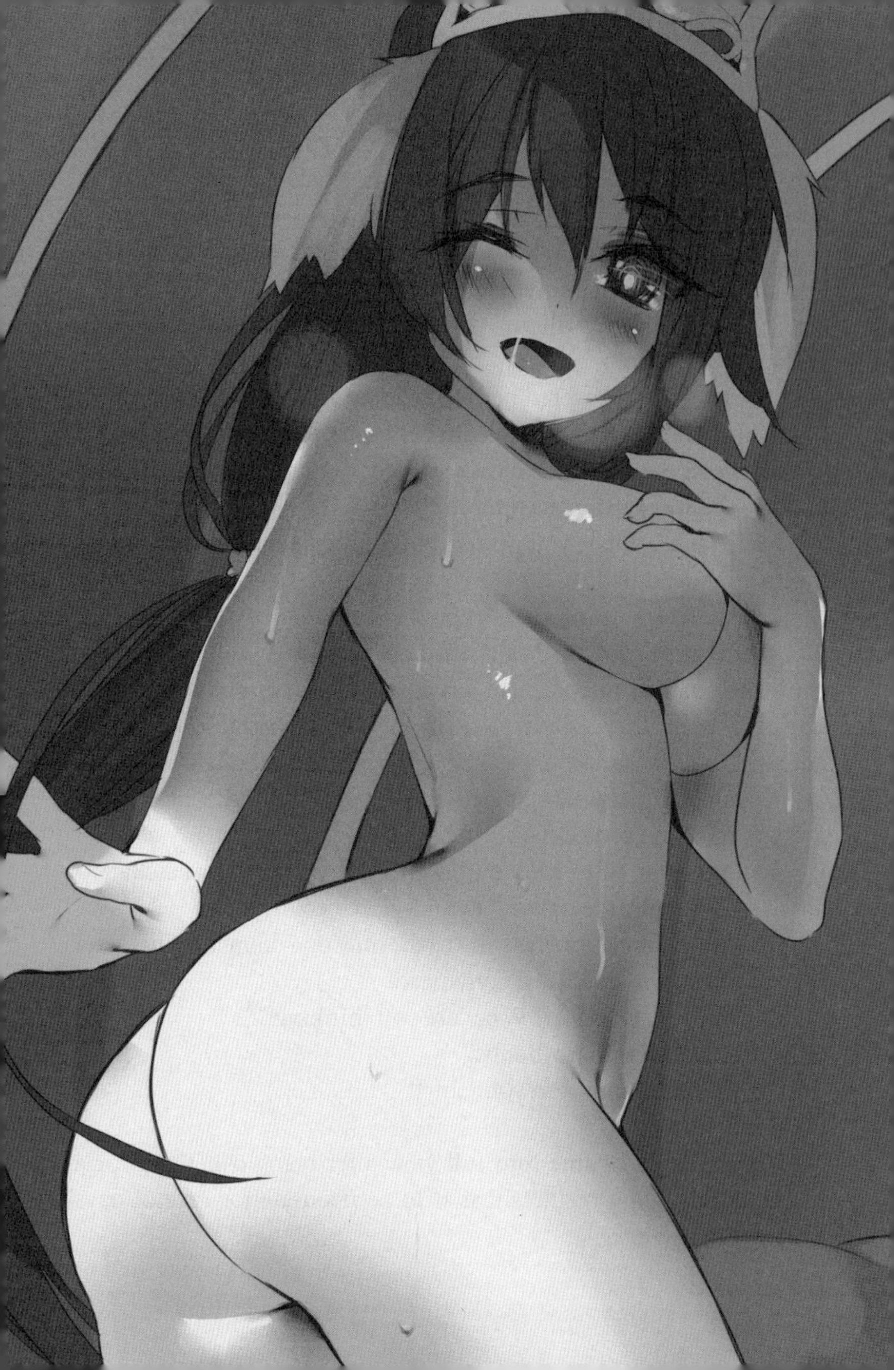

"Mmmm!" Rilitana stretched out her arms. "It feels so good! This wind! This sunlight! This freedom! Aaaah, being naked is wonderful!"

"…Ah, I, uhm, see…" Rem replied, dumbstruck. "I don't, erm, take my clothes off in public, so I wouldn't know…"

She didn't deny Rilitana's way of life either, but she couldn't restrain a shiver in her voice.

"Aaaah." Shera covered her flushed face with both hands.

Though she did peek out from between her fingers…

Rilitana seemed to have enjoyed their reactions, though, because she was getting even more cheerful.

"Heheheh… Once you get used to feeling people's stares on you, it gets kind of addicting."

"…No, I, erm, think that's enough."

Rem once had to walk through a village of Dark Elves completely naked to complete a magic ritual. Her body was quite sensitive back then. Perhaps Rem herself thought it could be addicting. Her expression was stiff at the moment, though.

"Ahaha…" Rilitana giggled awkwardly. "It's actually a bit awkward for everyone else to still have their clothes."

"…Even if all of us took our clothes off, we'd still feel awkward about walking outside naked," Rem declared coldly.

"You're right, it's lonely if you're the only one doing it!" Shera, on the other hand, nodded as if convinced.

"…Wait, Shera, what?! What are you thinking?!"

"It's tight around my boobs!"

"…Then just unbutton your shirt!"

"Woohoo!"

Shera's boobs came into full view after being contained for a long while, jiggling recklessly as if to compensate for several days' worth of dormancy.

"Aaaah, this is the best!"

"Doesn't it feel great, Shera?!"

"Yeah!"

It would have been such a serene, friendly conversation… if it weren't for the fact they were prancing around naked in the middle of the road.

"…This is a highway on the road to the capital, you know?" Rem said, her face as pale as a sheet. "There's no telling when someone might pass by and see you."

Rilitana's cheeks were flushed, and she rubbed her thighs together, fidgeting.

"Mmm… Going for verbal abuse already, Rem?"

"…I'm only stating the facts."

"Then you should be next."

"C'mon, Rem. Take off your clothes." Shera approached her.

"Are you a complete and total idiot?!" Rem raised her voice in shock. "I'm holding the reins… who do you think is driving this carriage?!"

"Then Paladin Captain, if you would? Or… would you like to join us, too?"

Diablo moved over to the driver's seat before the situation could go in an even stranger direction. Rilitana and Shera's breasts were bouncing all over the place, and Diablo honestly wasn't handling this well. He snatched the reins away from Rem.

"Hmph! I will handle the carriage. Leave it to me!"

"Diablo?!"

You have fun now… Diablo thought as Rem was being dragged back into the wagon. Not too long ago, Diablo had had his back turned while Rem and Shera were bathing. He couldn't sneak a peek back then, and the same held true now. This time didn't quite count since Shera had stripped right in front of his eyes, but... Diablo didn't have the nerve to watch the girls as they frolicked about in the wagon. He simply gripped the reins and kept his gaze fixed forward.

Ugh... I haven't changed a bit...

"No, stop... Aaah, don't take that off..." Rem's seductive yelping reached his ears. "Ah, aaah...! We're in broad daylight... Th-This isn't like bathing! Nnn, aaah, nnnng?!"

"My oh my... Rem, that's amazing."

"Whoa, look at the state you're in, Rem!"

He could hear Rilitana and Shera too.

"D-Doooon't..."

"It's fine, Rem... God will forgive us. We're all born naked, after all."

"She's right. What feels good is right, Rem."

"N-No, don't... Th-this... This feels... addictiiiiing!"

†

Thankfully, the whole debacle ended with no one else bearing witness to it, and Diablo's group was now close to the capital. Many carriages passed through this area, so even with a canopied carriage, they'd be seen. It wasn't as hot now, so Diablo thought they'd be fine, but...

Dusk washed over the sky. The fields around them were dyed in red, and ahead of them were tall, massive walls. Several spear-like towers were built into these walls.

It looks weird every time I look at it...

The capital, Seven Wall, looked largely different from how it appeared in *Cross Reverie*.

"When were these walls built again?" Diablo asked, thinking back to a conversation he once had with Lumachina.

"Hmm… When I was taken to the capital fourteen years ago, they weren't there… Ah, I think it was twelve years ago. That's when the current, sixth king of Lyferia, His Majesty Delouche Xandros, took to the throne and ordered for them to be built."

"The king of Lyferia…"

Diablo turned to look at the wagon. They weren't naked anymore. Rilitana looked at him composedly, as if nothing had happened. Except her skin seemed a touch more lustrous than it was before.

"We just need to pass through the gate, Paladin Captain."

"M-Mhm."

It was hard to face her pure smile after he'd seen her true nature. Shera was fast asleep. Maybe getting so excited had depleted all her strength. Frankly speaking, she was a sloth.

Did Shera even do anything on our journey to and from the southern frontier?

Diablo couldn't recall a single thing she actually did the whole trip. Well, she was the reason they met the Kobolds… but that's only because she was about to eat a venomous fruit. And she'd fought Gewalt, the Palace Knight… whom Rem ended up dispatching. And she'd had Solami fondle her butt, licked Diablo's finger, and stripped Rem naked…

This is the queen of the Elves…?

Seeing Shera snooze away with her belly exposed, Diablo grieved Greenwood's future.

Rem, on the other hand, sat in the wagon's corner. Having been stripped naked in public to the point where she screamed that it was 'addictiiiiing!' seemed to have had predictable effects, as she was mumbling to herself.

"Pull yourselves together, already," Diablo said dismissively. "We're almost to the capital."

"Kuh... So you didn't strip, did you... Huh?!" Rem's expression turned seriously all of a sudden and she leaped to the driver's seat. "Diablo, what's that?!"

"Hmm?!"

She was pointing in the city's direction. Rilitana covered her mouth with both hands.

"That's an army!" Diablo blurted out.

A large number of troops, more than Diablo had ever seen, left the capital's gate. Some were heavy infantry, covered in full-body armor. Others were cavaliers, with even their horses clad in mail. Gunners walked on, shouldering magi guns. Some soldiers transported large barrels.

And above them all flapped a banner Diablo remembered from *Cross Reverie* — a crown crossed with a sword.

"This is a military expedition. It's led by the king himself."

Which meant this was the Kingdom of Lyferia's primary army, with every soldier they could spare. The Order of Palace Knights was likely part of it, too.

Diablo had the ability to gauge how many enemies he was up against, but it was different when an army was involved. He couldn't even begin to imagine how many soldiers were walking there. It was likely more than fifty or sixty-thousand.

"...I've once seen an army of thirty-thousand," Rem moaned. "But this is likely more than three times that number."

"So it's almost one hundred-thousand?"

"...If not more."

Did they really mount this many soldiers against Diablo? He was expecting to fight the Palace Knights, but this was way more than he'd imagined. This would also mean they were aware of Diablo's approach to the capital. Did Rilitana betray them? No, it was hard to imagine, especially considering how she fooled around naked in a moving carriage earlier.

Maybe they were reported at a checkpoint? It was possible.

"Would they really send this big of a force, though?"

"...Something's odd, Diablo. This army is heading east."

Diablo's group was approaching the capital from the south.

"What could this mean?" Rilitana tilted her head curiously.

She was intelligent, but not when it came to military matters.

"...It means that army isn't setting out against us..." Rem answered.

Diablo sighed in relief internally, but didn't let his severe expression slip away.

Not that I can act all that dignified when I'm disguised as a woman...

"East of the Kingdom of Lyferia... isn't that the holy land of Vilaar?"

"...The Kingdom has signed a pact of non-aggression with its neighbors."

Them having signed a pact didn't mean it would necessarily be honored, though. That said, none of this carriage's passengers were in any position to discuss military or politics.

"Hmph... This is becoming annoying,"

"...What do we do, Diablo?"

"We hurry to the capital, of course!"

They couldn't lose their nerve now. If there was some ruckus going on, it was all the more reason not to leave Sylvie and Horn in the capital.

"It's going to shake!" Diablo grabbed the reins hard. "Hold on tight!"

Rilitana clung to the wagon as Rem gave a stern response.

"I'll be fine!"

"Let's go!"

As the carriage suddenly started shaking hard, Shera jerked awake with a surprised shout.

"Wh-What?! What happened?! Is something wrong?!"

No one bothered answering her questions, though. Sneaking one more glance at the army marching east, Diablo's group headed into the capital.

At the capital, Seven Wall, the southern gate was unusually crowded.

"Kh… What is the meaning of this?" Diablo raised his voice in irritation.

"…The other gates must be overcrowded since the army is using the eastern gate."

Many of the people lined up at the gate were traveling merchants. The ones leaving the capital were mostly entire families, fleeing west due to the coming conflict.

"…It does look like a war is going on," Rem said as she looked on at the commotion. "People tend to stock up on oil and food supplies during wartime, so their prices spike. I assume some sharp-eared merchants are buying those things in bulk from remote regions, where word of the war hasn't spread yet, and selling them for a profit here in the capital."

"Hmph. Taking advantage of a war to trade…"

"I'm sorry…" Rilitana hung her head. "If I had gathered information correctly at the checkpoints, maybe I'd have heard that war had broken out…"

"…That's not your fault," Rem consoled her. "We're the ones who needed to get past the checkpoints as fast as possible. You didn't have time to gather information."

She then turned to Diablo.

"…Diablo, maybe we should ask one of the merchants in line for information?"

Diablo almost nodded, but then shook his head.

"No, the High Priest should know more than any random merchant. Let's hurry to the Grand Cathedral."

"Understood."

"Let's go around the east gate and instead try the north one." Rilitana pointed to a point across the wall. "There should be a gate to the twelfth district, where the Grand Cathedral is."

"…I do hope we make it in time."

It was nearly sunset, and the gates closed at nightfall. It would stay stubbornly shut no matter how many people came and demanded to be let through. Seven Wall was a massive city, larger than any city should be in such a medieval world. Even going halfway through it via carriage took a considerable amount of time. By the time they reached the twelfth district's gate, it was already dark.

Much to their surprise, however, the gate was still open. There was a crowd of soldiers, and standing in the center was a girl clad in a red and white robe. The High Priest, Lumachina!

But what was the High Priest, who usually resided in the Inner Sanctum, doing here in front of a crowded gate?

Diablo looked over her three times, but it was definitely Lumachina, surrounded by believers. At both of her sides stood knights in blue armor — probably Paladins. Diablo couldn't see their faces due to the wavering light of the torches.

"Lumachinaaaaaaaaaaa!" Shera waved her hand.

"Are you completely and utterly stupid, Shera?!" Rem hurriedly grabbed her by the ear and dragged her back.

"Ow, ouch! My ear! Not the ear!"

"…This is the main gate to the Grand Cathedral! If you call the High Priest by her name here, you'll be arrested for irreverence!"

"Uuu…"

"…Besides, with things being this loud, she can't hear you shouting at her from this far away."

"Then let's walk over to her."

They didn't have much of a choice. Diablo quickly adjusted his outfit. They might have to discard their carriage, but going forward without Rem, Shera, and Rilitana worried him. Rem looked down at her own appearance with an embarrassed face. Right now she looked like a Pantherian boy.

"…I'm not sure Lumachina will recognize us even if we do address her directly."

"Ahaha, you're right." Shera, who stood next to her, looked like an Elf boy.

Diablo was in disguise too, of course. He was dressed like a somewhat thuggish lady.

Ugh… To think I have to see her again while looking like this.

"That's what I'm here for," Rilitana promised, "I'll explain everything to her."

Diablo decided to leave things to her, since she had many acquaintances in the upper echelons of the church.

†

Diablo and his group got off the carriage and approached the gate, weaving their way through the crowd. Apparently Lumachina was arguing with someone. The person opposing her was a man in fancy armor — apparently some sort of high-ranking military official.

"With all due respect, just what are you thinking, Your Eminence?! The gate should have been closed a long time ago already!"

"My apologies, but if only for just today…"

"I have a responsibility to keep the capital safe! You may be the highest official of the church, but I can't allow you to do as you please!"

"But…"

"We have the Empire attacking us from the east, and that Demon revolting against us in the south! And to add to all that, there are rumors of a Demon Lord to the west! Even the capital cannot be considered safe at this point!"

A Demon revolting in the south? Does he mean me?!

Apparently the army had set out because some empire attacked Lyferia. Diablo thought back to *Cross Reverie*'s lore. An empire east of Lyferia's…

The Gelmed Empire, right…?

It was mentioned in the game, but only a handful of times. That was mostly because the Gelmed Empire was actually the setting for another game made by the same developer as *Cross Reverie* — the simulated life game called *Girls' Arms*.

And they're the ones who've invaded Lyferia…?

The two games had a limited-time collaboration event, but nothing remotely like that happened in the game.

I did play Girls' Arms *for a while… But was there anything about them invading?*

"…Aren't those rumors about a Demon Lord to the west concerning? What if it's Klem?"

"No way!" Shera exclaimed in a voice choked with tears.

Rilitana didn't know about Klem and simply looked perplexed.

"It could be, but there's no point worrying about that right now."

They were close enough for their voices to reach Lumachina now. Still, yelling to greet the High Priest would be disrespectful. But since they hesitated, Lumachina's guards noticed them first.

"You there! Who are you?!" A Human female guard. Her voice was somehow familiar, and indeed, she was someone they knew: Tria, the paladin. A nostalgic face, indeed; Rem had once received a key from Gewalt when he defected from the church, allowing her to free Tria from her prison in the confessional room. At the time, she was so weakened she couldn't even stand on her own, but apparently she'd recovered since. She was once again standing as a dignified paladin.

"…It's good to see she's all better now." Rem smiled with relief.

"Yep, yep! It's great!" Shera grinned, too.

"Mmm? Who might you be…?"

Rem and Shera were disguised, after all, and the torch light was far back. Tria didn't notice who they were in the darkness. Of course, Diablo was disguised, too.

I feel like using the paladin captain's mark now would just complicate things.

Rilitana stepped forward. Diablo concluded that letting her handle things would make everything quicker.

"It's been a long while, Miss Tria."

"Oh… You're Lady Rilitana! What brings you here?"

"I believe it was to lead the people Her Eminence was waiting for, and for whom she kept the gate open."

Tria raised her brows in surprise.

"I, uhm, pardon me. We kept the gate open at the High Priest's order, but we weren't told why she wanted to keep it open…"

"My… Is that right?"

"To be more exact, the High Priest told us 'we mustn't close the gate,' though she could not say why."

So it was just intuition?

"…That does sound like Lumachina." Rem shrugged.

"Ahaha… Yeah, she can be like that," Shera said.

"Her Eminence would indeed do that. I'm sure God has guided her. I'm sure He's told her of our coming arrival."

"Understood!" Tria directed a single suspicious glance in Diablo's direction and returned to Lumachina's side. His disguise was too good, it seemed. No one realized who he was.

Lumachina was told of their arrival, and turned to look in their direction. Her gaze met with his. He was cross-dressing, and really well at that, so he felt pretty embarrassed.

How am I supposed to greet her like this, anyway…?

He had come to the High Priest for help, so would he be able to keep a low profile? Common sense stated he should, but between being a Demon Lord and the incarnation of God, Diablo had all sorts of airs to put on. Lowering his head would get in the way of his role playing!

Still, he couldn't talk down to the High Priest when they were surrounded by believers. Lumachina had her own dignity to keep, after all. And stating he was a Demon Lord when he was surrounded by soldiers would be… well, suicide!

Alright! Diablo steeled himself. *I'll leave everything to Rem and hang back quietly!*

Diablo prided himself on this decision. Compared to back when he would have just declared himself a Demon Lord anyway and gotten them all into trouble, this was a feat of impressive character growth! No, this was even a show of social awareness! Did he just conquer his communication issues?!

But his master plan of having Rem smooth things over with Lumachina crumbled in an instant. Surprisingly, Lumachina pushed past the important-looking military official, turned to quiet her guards, and ran over to them with a desperate expression.

"Lumachina?!" Rem exclaimed in shock.

"Whaaa?!" Shera's eyes widened in surprise, too.

Rilitana stepped back and lowered her head reverently. Lumachina ignored everyone and approached Diablo, jumping at him and catching him in an embrace.

"Lord Diablo!"

"Wha?!" Diablo exclaimed in surprise. He didn't expect her to just cling to him like that... Plus, she was soft. A peculiar aroma wafted from her, mixed in with the slight scent of sweat. Lumachina's body shivered slightly as she clung to him.

Everyone around them was dumbstruck. The High Priest had suddenly leapt onto and hugged someone. They were so stunned by what had happened that one might have suspected they'd been struck with a petrification spell.

Tria was the first to come to.

"The High Priest will now return to the Inner Sanctum!"

She was young, but also capable of making judgments on her own and acting on them. An unusual trait for a member of an organization.

Diablo picked up Lumachina, who still clung to him.

"It doesn't look like you're just happy to see me again..."

"I-I'm sorry... I lost my composure..."

"Stay as you are."

Picking up on Diablo's intent, Rem raised her voice.

"The High Priest is not feeling well! Please, clear the way!"

People had a tendency of seeing what they want to see. And so, when they were told that Lumachina had collapsed, it made more sense to them than her suddenly hugging someone.

The man who had argued with Lumachina earlier turned a suspicious look in their direction. Upon getting a look at the man's face, Diablo very nearly let out an 'ugh' despite himself.

He had met and argued with this man during his audience with the king of Lyferia. If he recalled, he was a Major in the military. Of all the military officials it could be, it was the one who had interacted with Diablo the longest.

Dammit! If he exposes me, this is gonna become that much more annoying!

And that wasn't even the worst part. If he found out Diablo was crossdressing, his Demon Lord-ly dignity would be ruined!

Diablo himself had completely forgotten his name, but it was Harold William. He was a thirty-year-old Major and a Human of a famous noble house. All things considered, he was a fairly accomplished man.

Except his talents were suited less for combat and more for behind-the-scenes work. His role in this campaign was defending the city and managing the supply line, so he was left behind in the capital.

Harold gave Diablo a long look, and then parted his lips to say…

"…Gorgeous."

"Huh?" Diablo replied with his natural voice.

It didn't reach Harold's ears, though.

"Perfectly molded features, fair, white skin, a robust figure. Never have I laid eyes on such a lovely woman!"

"Hey, uhh, you're…"

Incidentally, Diablo owed his 'fair, white skin' at this time to the vast amounts of powder applied to his face to hide his Demon tattoos.

"Please, marry me! Aaah, no, at least tell me your name!"

What in the absolute hell is this guy saying?!

As the Major stepped closer, Shera stepped in between them.

"Sowwy, sowwy! We're carrying Lady Lumachina away right now! No getting in the way, bub!"

"Ugh… Right you are. I cannot believe myself…" Harold said.

He was a man of nobility, after all. He was thoroughly educated to prioritize caring for a woman that felt unwell.

"Your Eminence, do take care of yourself." He stepped aside.

And while directing a rather fiery gaze at Diablo, he gave an exemplary salute, as one might expect of an officer.

As they walked away…

"…That one will come to the church looking for you," Rem said coldly. "I would gamble my bottom frith on it."

"Good grief…" Diablo winced. "This is an entirely different kind of annoying situation…"

†

Diablo, Rem, and Shera placed Lumachina in the large carriage that was prepared for her and climbed in. Rilitana and the Paladin Tria hurried after them and got on, as well.

"My apologies." Lumachina bowed her head deeply.

The carriage took off, shaking and jolting lightly as it did.

"Give me a second," Diablo said, removing his wig and dress.

He re-equipped his usual cloak, the 《Sojourn of Darkness》, and tried to wipe the white powder off of his face with his hand, though some of it still lingered.

Don't joke around with me, I just got proposed to by a freaking guy!

Rem and Shera stayed in their male outfits. Diablo placed his disguise in his pouch, but the girls' clothes stayed behind in their carriage. They'd have to go back to collect them later. Assuming it wasn't taken away by someone, given that they'd left it outside the gate…

Having mostly gone back to his usual attire, Diablo crossed his arms and leaned his body against the back of his seat before finally regarding Lumachina's words.

"Hmph… Carrying you is child's play. Forget that, however. What happened?"

She wasn't just overjoyed at their reunion. She had acted far too emotional for that.

"Yes… I don't know what I should do…" Lumachina said with a shaking voice. "I prayed and prayed for someone to come and save me…"

Rem and Shera listened to her with severe expressions.

"So I prayed to be saved…" Lumachina continued, "And then the Lord extended his words upon me, and said a hand of salvation would be extended to me from the direction of the north gate…"

Had anyone else said they'd 'heard God's words', no one would believe them. But in this girl's case, it seemed to be true. And indeed, Diablo did arrive through the northern gate.

Though it's actually us who came to her for help here…

"What happened? Could you start by explaining that?"

It would be much easier if it was just a quest with some clear objective like slaying a large monster or finding a rare item.

"I-I've seen a most horrifying dream." Lumachina hung her head.

"Oh?"

"A dream of this capital being enveloped in flames…"

"I see."

So she dreamt of the Gelmed Empire from the east attacking the capital…?

"…If that was a prophetic dream, then it's a terrible thing to see." Rem furrowed her brows. "But I don't think this is a situation Diablo can resolve on his own, though…?"

"Yes." Lumachina understood that much.

The Kingdom of Lyferia had sent out an army of over 100,000 men, along with the Palace Knights. And if the capital would still be set aflame, then that means…

A losing war? Okay, yeah, I don't want any part in that!

He wasn't in service to the Kingdom of Lyferia to begin with, and if he was associated with any place, it was Greenwood, since he was their king. He wanted to gather his comrades and leave as soon as possible, taking Lumachina along if it was necessary. Could that really be called 'a hand of salvation'?

"I prioritize Her Eminence's wellbeing over the safety of the capital," Tria the paladin said. "If it is necessary, I am prepared to flee the city with her."

It seemed she felt the same way as Diablo. Lumachina's facial expression, however, didn't seem very comfortable with this idea.

"We must see to it that it will not be necessary."

"Of course, we all pray for the kingdom's army to emerge victorious. But in case they don't, the paladins have their duty to consider."

Now that's a real paladin.

All the other paladins he'd run into were corrupt villains, so Tria came across as all the more noble. Diablo almost wanted to applaud her.

"You still push yourself so hard, Lady Lumachina," Rilitana said.

"That's not true… This is hardly enough."

"I think you're fulfilling your role as High Priest perfectly well. The only things Priests like us can do is offer up prayers to God… Can you not let these people take care of the rest?"

She was like a mother chiding her daughter.

"Yes… You're right." Lumachina nodded.

†

The Inner Sanctum came into sight. On the ground level it was just a small chapel, but the actual Inner Sanctum was a structure floating in the sky above it. It was said God created it in the age of myths, meaning it had a history that predated the Kingdom of Lyferia.

Put another way, the Inner Sanctum wasn't built in the capital, but rather the capital was built around the Inner Sanctum.

And Diablo had once fired several flashy attacks spells at a place with such worldwide significance, even if it was only for the sake of playing the part of Demon Lord. With that considered, visiting it again like this was actually kind of awkward…

Lumachina seemed to have calmed down a bit. Her expression was much softer than it was when they'd initially reunited.

"...Lumachina, I hate to ask this as soon as we've arrived, but could you do us a favor?" Rem said, going straight to the heart of the matter.

"Yes?"

"..Sylvie and Horn are here in the capital."

"Yes, they are."

Lumachina was familiar with both of them, especially with Horn. The two had adventured together once, and it was with Lumachina's recommendation that Horn was admitted to the Sorcerer's Academy. She was now technically Horn's guardian.

"...Actually, we've broken away from the Kingdom of Lyferia. If possible, we would like to secure Horn and Sylvie's safety."

"So it is true... I've heard the rumors."

"...This may end up compromising your position," Rem said apologetically.

"That's nonsense. You've all opposed the entirety of the church to help me once before, haven't you?"

"...That's true, but..."

"Right now, I'm not just a nominal decoration for the church. I am the High Priest. Even if His Majesty were to directly order it, I would never hand you over as criminals."

"...Thank you."

"I do think you'll be relieved quite soon, Miss Rem." Lumachina gave a small smile.

"Huh?"

Their carriage reached the area directly below the Inner Sanctum. This was a sector no one but those chosen by the church could enter. Diablo and his group followed Lumachina to the levitating platform and entered the floating Inner Sanctum.

†

"Boss?!"

Two people they didn't expect to see were waiting for them in a large guest room; both of them Grasswalkers — Horn and Sylvie.

"How's it hangin', Diablo? ♪" Sylvie asked, her rabbit ears moving to and fro. "Rem and Shera too, it's such a relief to see you all made it to the capital."

Grasswalkers were a race that retained a childlike appearance no matter how many years passed. However, Horn really was thirteen, while Sylvie's age was… well… unknown.

Diablo did know she'd participated in the Great War 30 years ago, and was already a veteran adventurer at that time. She'd even hinted she was looking to retire as the guildmaster of the adventurer's guild, so maybe she was that old.

Sylvie aside, Horn seemed quite taken aback by Rem and Shera's crossdressing.

"Horn?! Sylvie?!" Rem's eyes widened. "Why are you here…?!"

"She brought them here." Lumachina gestured further into the room.

They looked that way, and their gaze fell on a red-headed girl sitting on one of the sofas. She rose to her feet briskly, an all-too-perfect smile on her lips, as usual. A flawless, borderline-artificial smile.

"Alicia?!" Shera exclaimed.

"Yes, it's been quite some time, Miss Shera. Miss Rem as well, and of course — Sir Diablo."

"…I didn't think we'd find you here." Rem rushed to her side.

"I would have liked to let you know, but after your battle in Caliture, I lost track of your whereabouts."

Alicia wasn't just an Imperial Knight, she was also a noble family's daughter, and had her own independent intelligence network.

"Siding with Kobolds does feel like something you might do, Sir Diablo."

"They were really nice!" Shera chimed in.

And indeed, they weren't bad folk.

There was a knock on the guest room door. The paladin Tria strode over and opened the door. A pleasant scent wafted into the room.

"Lady Lumachina and her guests, please make yourselves at home... We've prepared supper. I'm sure you have plenty to discuss, so please, help yourselves."

They gratefully accepted the offer. Many dishes were placed all over the table on top of wooden plates. After all the funds the former Cardinal Authority embezzled, the church had collapsed economically. They elected to sell its silverware, and other such expensive furnishings, to help ease their financial trouble.

Now even the High Priest was eating off of wooden plates, just like the commoners. They were served thin soup with some beans, steamed chicken with fruit sauce, grilled whitefish with mustard, black bread, mushrooms cooked in garlic oil... and the like.

It was a frugal meal, but there was plenty of effort and skill put into making it palatable. The flavor was richer than Diablo expected — apparently the salt was doing its job well. Diablo and his group had lived off of preserved food for the duration of their long journey, so they found the meal to be quite delectable.

Rem placed plenty of sauce on her steamed chicken and brought it to her mouth.

"…Alicia, you brought Sylvie and Horn here?" she asked after savoring the flavor for a long moment.

"It may have been impertinent of me, I admit."

"It was prettttyyy dangerous," Sylvie said without a trace of tension in her voice.

Year 165 of the Lyferian calendar, 24th day of the second month...

The kingdom's army of 110,000 soldiers clashed with the Empire of Gelmed's forces. The engagement took place in the Grutalia plains, located halfway between the capital, Seven Wall, and the eastern citadel city of Kenstone.

It was known as an old battlefield, where countless battles had taken place some 300 years ago. Rusted equipment and crumbled skeletons littered the ground. The empty eye sockets of their cracked skulls seemed to beckon the new arrivals to become their new companions. It was an eerie place, enough to strike even the most experienced of warriors silent.

If Diablo was here, his impression of the place would have been different. "This battlefield was featured in *Cross Reverie*. It was for some limited-time ranking event... It was meant for entire parties, so it was pretty challenging for a solo player... I cleared it, though."

The ones to start the fighting were Lyferia's army.

"Fire!"

With the commander's order, their large summons roared. The improved version of the 《Salamander》 summons, 《Gore Salamanders》, as well as 《Red Hydras》 and 《Devil Eyes》 were all present — all over level 60 and optimized for high firepower bombardment.

They fired a volley capable of reducing even armored infantry to dust. However, the Gelmed Empire's soldiers simply raised their large shields, advancing through the flames. Lyferia's mages were dumbstruck.

"I-Impossible!"

"Charge!"

The Gelmed Empire's army rushed toward them.

"Ooooooh!"

"Don't let them push you back!"

Lyferia's commanding officers barked orders at their soldiers, but the difference in their equipment was too vast. The Empire's soldiers employed magimatic weapons, after all. They had spears that could tear enemies apart with a mere graze, and shields capable of rendering attacks useless. Lyferia's soldiers had some unique equipment, but it was all precious and rare. Only a select handful of soldiers had them.

Bad news was flooding into Lyferia's military headquarters.

"Your Majesty! Our forces are being routed!"

"It can't be…"

How could they be overwhelmed so thoroughly? Lyferia's king, Delouche Xandros, felt his field of vision contort softly. If he weren't sitting on a chair at the time, he'd have crumbled to his feet.

"Ugh… Someone! Anyone! Push them back! Claim the head of one of the enemy's commanders and turn this battle around… Don't we have that kind of hero on our side?!"

Delouche looked around his staff officers, but they all cast down their eyes, refusing to meet his gaze.

"Ugh…"

"Why?! Answer me!" He cornered one of the officers. "Our Kingdom of Lyferia has fought off the Demon Lord so many times!

The Empire might be powerful, but they're not stronger than the Fallen!"

"…If I may humbly speak, Your Majesty… The Fallen are limited in numbers. They're not organized in formations, either. Compared to us, the Empire's army is far more organized."

"Are you calling our soldiers a disorderly mob?!"

"A-A hero might be able to…" he stammered, when Delouche suddenly jolted.

"That's right! Alan, the hero! What about the Palace Knights?! Where's Noah?!"

"Duke Gibun already went to the front lines with the Order of Palace Knights."

"What…?"

"The enemy has Magimatic Sols, and normal weapons can't do any damage to them. Without warriors with equipment capable of penetrating their barriers, fighting them is just sending our men to be killed. With that in mind, Duke Gibun said the Palace Knights should strike the first blow."

"…He did mention something like that…"

"The operation went as you ordered, Your Majesty."

The staff officers looked at each other, unable to say anything. What was this long war council for? He only raised his voice, but he didn't have any idea about the strategy they were employing — Delouche was well aware that his status as king was entirely nominal. That was fine in peacetime, but during times of war, he wasn't dependable.

"So you're saying… This is our situation *after* we've sent in our trump cards?" Delouche hung his head. "Is the Kingdom of Lyferia really that weak?"

They had over twice the enemy's numbers, but they were still being overwhelmed. The staff officers exchanged gazes. Now wasn't the time to wallow in regret. The front lines had collapsed, and they had no play that would change the situation. Their only remaining option was to retreat.

If they didn't run in time, their headquarters might end up being attacked by the enemy. The awful idea that the Empire's soldiers might be attacking them sent shivers down their spines... Still, the sounds of fighting were still far off.

"...What's going to happen?" one of the staff officers asked.

"I-I'm sure the Empire's soldiers are getting fatigued by now," another said, smiling bitterly. "We do have over twice their number in soldiers."

"So the Kingdom's soldiers are hanging on. Good! If we take advantage of our numbers and surround them, we might still turn this around."

"Reorganize our forces at once!"

But as the staff officers were speaking in an animated fashion, a scream tore into their ears, along with a heavy, unfamiliar metallic sound.

"What's going on?!" Delouche called out.

The next moment... the heavy infantry surrounding the headquarters were thrown into the air like dry leaves.

"Gaaah?!"

A massive suit of metallic armor appeared beyond the crowd of soldiers. Its exterior was a sleek, yellowish color, and it carried swords in opposite ways.

"*Ahahaha!*" The high-pitched voice of a child echoed around them. "*I~ found~ the king~!*"

The pilot of this Magimatic Sol was Toaha — the Lamia girl who was said to be the unit's ace. The knights surrounded Delouche.

"Stay away from His Majesty!" one of them said, brandishing a spear.

The yellow Magimatic Sol crossed its blades in both its hands.

"It's all point~less! You can't stop my Elrenoss with those things. It's check and mate~ ♪"

She swung her massive blades, and the knights' blood gushed through the air.

"How dare you treat me with such insolence?!" Delouche screamed at her. "I'm the king of Lyferia! Ruler of the raceeeeeeeeeees!"

"Uh, sure?"

Toaha imagined swinging a blade into his head without so much as a sliver of hesitation. The thin, minute terminals, coiled all over and into her body, reaching as far as her brain, transmitted those thoughts to her unit faster than her nerve pulses traveled. The magimatic armor instantaneously, faithfully, and accurately executed its pilot's orders. The two blades swung down toward Delouche's shoulders...

And slammed into the earth.

In a single moment, which passed by in an instant... Lyferia's crown clattered to the ground and into a spreading puddle of red.

Delouche Xandros was reduced to a splatter of gore. Just blood and flesh.

The yellowish Magimatic Sol, Elrenoss, wiped its blades.

"Aaaaaand, done. ♪"

"Uuu... Aaah..."

The staff officers, who could only watch from the sidelines, were splashed with their king's blood. Their gazes were fixed on Toaha.

"*Right, so what was I supposed to do aside from off the king? Hmm... Aira, do you reeeead? I'm done here, so what's next?*"

They could hear some voice, muffled and crackling with noise. She was speaking to someone. They could clearly hear Toaha's responses, though.

"*What, Saya's in danger?! What is she thinkiiiing~? Fiiine, I'll go back!*"

She seemed to be ignoring the surrounding staff officers. The Magimatic Sol turned its back and began to leave. Officers burning with a desire to avenge their king stood in its way, but...

"Damn you!"

"*Out of my way!*"

She easily beat them down. Watching the Magimatic Sol leave, one of the staff officers fell to his knees. His sword slipped from his fingers and fell to the ground.

"It's all over... The Kingdom of Lyferia... is done for..."

The king was crushed to bits. Magimatic Sols marched through casually, even with the kingdom's most skilled heavy infantry standing in their way.

"Uuu... Aaaah..." The staff officer wept openly. "This is even more one-sided than when we fought the Demon Lord..."

†

Without a king to protect, the Lyferian army was being routed. The Gelmed Empire's army launched a pursuit, and the battlefield became an echo chamber of screams of agony.

But one group was retreating rather composedly. A large dragon carriage — a carriage towed by an earth dragon — was moving along faster than a messenger on horseback, despite its size.

Sitting at its driver's seat and holding the reins was a large man with black-rimmed glasses, his hair parted to the side. His features were intellectual, but his body was a large lump of muscles.

This was Maximum Abrams, the captain of the Order of Palace Knights.

"Sir Noah, it seems the king has died in battle."

Sitting next to him was a beautiful person of androgynous appearance — Duke Noah Gibun, who also doubled as a high-ranking general.

"So it seems… Coupled with how poor the situation is, this must be why the soldiers' morale is so crippled."

News of the king's demise had likely spread among the army. A boy peeked his head out of the window leading into the carriage's compartment. He was a Dwarf with golden, spiky hair, and this generation's hero, Alan.

"Are you sure that was all right? Isn't protecting the king kind of our job? I could have kept fighting, you know."

A brown-haired woman then poked her face out beside him. She had a mark extending from her forehead down to her cheek. She was a Demon girl, and carried a magi gun on her shoulder.

"Sir Noah doesn't make mistakes, blockhead. It's not like his name is Alan or something!"

Someone was sitting behind her in the wagon, his arms crossed. An Elf man, dressed in a red trenchcoat with a black longsword dangling from his waist: Thanatos the Undying.

"…And yet, we are in need of explanation. The captain may be satisfied without one, but I am not exactly fine with running away when I was not even defeated."

Sitting opposite him was a child — or rather, a Grasswalker girl who looked like one.

"Ohoh?" she said, dangling her feet in a bored gesture. "So our good friend Thanatos here will disobey Sir Noah's orders unless he gets an explanation, huh? There's that rebellious spirit for you. So cool~"

"Tch... I said nothing of the sort."

"Then you don't need a reason now, do you?"

"It would change my intro line, don't you see?! If I don't know my position or objective, it could create discrepancies later on. That would force me to go with something more generic and vague. Do you think a generic intro line would make my soul burn bright?"

"Sorry, buddy, my soul is noncombustible, so I don't really follow... "

"Right!" Alan exclaimed with a clenched fist. "You get it, Thanatos! If we don't know what's going on, we just can't get into the right mood, you know?!"

A Pantherian girl sitting at the back of the carriage quipped at him, "I don't think I've ever seen you 'not in the right mood' when it comes to battles, Alan. If anything, you keep fighting even when people tell you to stop."

"Ahahaha!" Alan turned red with a smug face. "Keep giving me compliments and you'll make me blush!"

"He's a moron," the Grasswalker girl poked at him. "Moron detector going off the charts."

Back at the driver's seat, Maximum Abrams knitted his brows.

"Their words have truth to them. If we don't know what position we're in, it could cause problems. In Alan's case, he'd pick unnecessary fights with people."

"I suppose that would be troublesome..." Noah smiled wryly. "The situation is somewhat complicated. Your orders were changed suddenly, so it makes sense you'd be confused."

"So this wasn't according to plan?"

"Yes... I suppose now would be the right time to talk. It will take us a few days to reach our destination even with an earth dragon's speed."

"Then please speak," Maximum said, turning his gaze forward as he waited for Noah to begin.

"Due to certain circumstances, I possess knowledge of a civilization far more advanced than Lyferia."

"Yes."

"I call it the 《Godsent Gift》. Using this higher-order knowledge, I climbed up to the rank of duke, and gained effective power over the Kingdom of Lyferia... I might have even been made royalty in the future."

"I thought that might eventually happen."

"However, after all of this, I've come to realize something. I am powerless."

"You have power matching the King of Lyferia and command the Order of Palace Knights, and you're still powerless?" Maximum tilted his head. "Do you perhaps mean that in comparison to the Empire's Magimatic Sols?"

"No... I didn't account for them, but... they were just the trigger."

"In which case?"

"A community of people can be a troublesome thing. Even a despotic king can't control everything freely. For example, if one wants to change taxation, they need the nobles' approval. The same holds true for the justice system, the education system, the currency, social status, logistics, medicine, the military's composition! Every single thing you might try to change has multiple layers, protected by the vested interests of the church and nobles."

"Even for the king, eh…"

"I've tried so many things…"

"The church's takeover looked like it might be successful."

"The Cardinal Authority's self-interests went too far. I should have taken measures against them sooner… Still, I never expected the High Priest to return alive."

"The end result was fine though, was it not? The current High Priest is an upright, upstanding person, skilled at performing miracles."

"And thanks to that, the church's structure was made more solid, and now we can't interfere with them. Looking at it in the long run, it pushed the reform back by 50 years."

"…This is a complicated matter."

"Whatever the case, I've realized something. One can't change the feudal system from above. The change has to come from either the outside or the bottom up. And so, I thought I would give the commoners power."

"I see."

"But, this world has magic. There's too much of a gap between an untrained commoner and a high-level soldier."

"Naturally. I'm confident I'd be able to win even if a whole city were to challenge me."

"Yes…" Noah nodded at Maximum's calm analysis.

"But I have one question. Is it truly that necessary to change the country's systems?"

"If you didn't know better, you might think this is the obvious, natural course of things, yes… The discrimination and poverty are quite severe here. Only a small fraction of nobles live in wealth, while commoners die like dogs. It's unforgivable."

"I thought you were of a noble family."

"…I guess there's little point to keeping it a secret…" Noah gave a thin smile. "I'm actually of common birth. I merely used my knowledge to acquire riches as a merchant. I then bought the position of a poor regional noble family's deceased eldest son. I assumed the identity of a man who hardly ever went outside."

Selling noble titles was outlawed in Lyferia, and a commoner couldn't join the nobility even through adoption. Assuming a noble's name was absolutely a criminal act.

Not that there was a king left alive to judge one for it now…

"Quite the surprise," Maximum said plainly, his gaze fixed forward.

"You don't look surprised to me."

"To be fair, I had my slight doubts… You look nothing like your parents, milord."

"Heheh… Then I think this one will really catch you off-guard. My true father was a bandit who was beaten to death by a regional knight. My mother was a prostitute that died from illness by the wayside. As an infant, I couldn't save either of them."

"It… certainly doesn't seem like you're jesting, milord," Maximum said, his eyes wide with surprise.

Smirking in satisfaction at his response, Noah continued.

"I thought… I could change this country by gaining power and authority. But now I know that I could become king, yet that would still be impossible."

Abrams responded with contemplative silence. "If a reform from above is impossible, and a revolution from the bottom up won't happen either, it must come from the outside. If an enemy powerful enough to deprive the nobles of their military appears, it could create a hole large enough to change the country's national policy."

Maximum then gasped in realization.

"The Demon Overlord?!"

"Even I can't control that thing's revival so freely... All I did was direct His Majesty to focus on fortifying the capital."

"I did think it strange we didn't send reinforcements to the west... So that was your motive for that."

By the time the Demon Overlord Modinaram would attack, Noah wanted to be ready, or at least close to ready, to subvert the State. Things didn't go as planned, however.

"I never thought it would be defeated in Faltra."

"Diablo."

"What is that man thinking?!" Noah grimaced. "He has so much power, but he's completely and utterly trackless! Just when I thought he'd press the High Priest for gratitude, he goes off to become king of a small country like Greenwood. And when I thought that was his angle, he saves Faltra."

"And reports say he recently fought the forces of Caliture's governor for some Kobolds... Gewalt was seriously injured by that."

"I don't understand him!"

"But he's strong. A dangerous man, certainly."

"Yes, I saw that perfectly well during our audience with him. He's not someone to needlessly meddle with, and we can't make him obey us, either. I doubt it's possible for me to even have a discussion with him."

"So he's not like us, in that regard."

It hadn't even been a year since the Order of Palace Knights was assembled, but it already felt nostalgic. A faraway look played over Noah's features.

"The imperial knights are all nobles, or the children of nobles. That's why I instigated His Majesty to limit their authority and organize the Palace Knights... I gathered all of you, who were shunned for being demis, and gave you legendary gear to use."

"Yes... Though our being shunned wasn't entirely due to our races."

Alan was a combat junkie, while Thanatos spoke in peculiar ways. The others all had quirks that made them incompatible with acting in a group. Maximum realized they only functioned together because Noah had gathered them.

"I've always had the Devil's luck..." Noah smiled. "When my parents passed away, I was picked up by merchants. When my business flourished, a family of poor nobles became my clients, and their son, who just happened to be the same age as me, passed away. And this time, just as my reform was coming to a stalemate, the Empire invades."

"Was Lyferia losing the war part of your calculations?"

"Didn't I just say that? If something can't be changed from the top down or from the bottom up, something from outside must be what shakes things."

"True... But are you sure this is a good idea? The Empire of Gelmed is one to enslave the people of the territories it conquers."

It seemed to clash with Noah's ideals of a country without discrimination or poverty.

"Of course, I don't intend to let them have their way." Noah nodded.

It seemed he'd already decided on what he had to do. Maximum was convinced, at that moment, that this person could see far further ahead than he and his comrades.

"I will follow you wherever you go, milord. I will be your blade."

"Heheh... Reliable words. Oh, right, right. Might as well share one more secret with you, while we're in the mood for shocking revelations."

"Yes?"

Noah removed his white mantle and undid the front of his uniform's top.

"The real me is neither innocent, nor a duke... Nor even a man."

Noah's chest was visibly plump.

"Ah...?!"

Maximum averted his gaze in shock, nearly driving the dragon carriage off the road. Out of everyone listening in on the pair's conversation in silence from inside the compartment, the Demon girl raised her voice in a scream.

"No waaaaay!"

"Are you for real? What about your balls?! Where're your balls?!"

Alan reached his hand for Noah's crotch, only for the Grasswalker girl to slap it away. Noah, meanwhile, was laughing so hard she had to hold onto her stomach.

The Palace Knights' carriage made its way to the west.

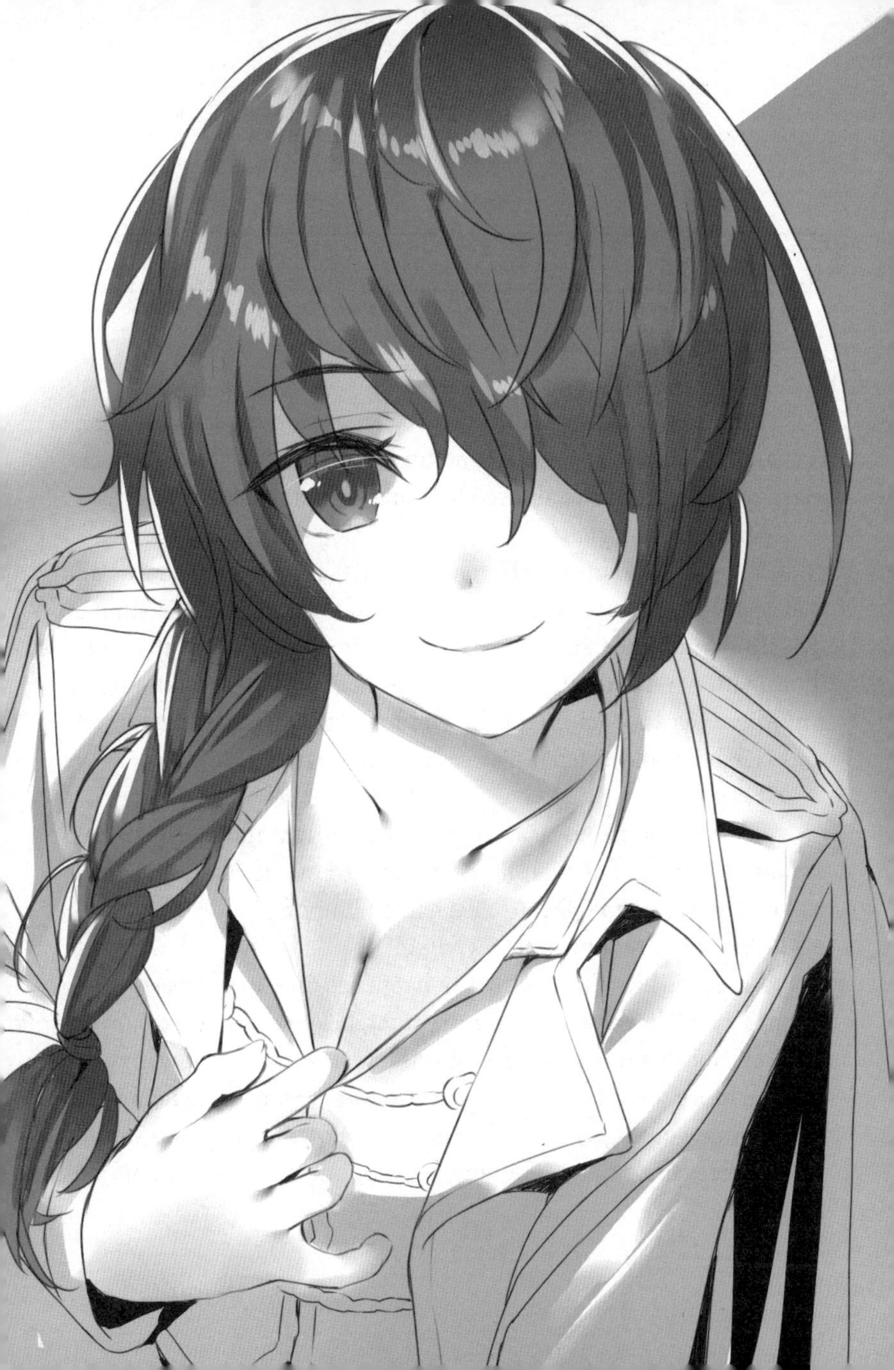

Chapter 4 The Capital Ablaze

A few days went by.

That night, Diablo lay on the bed in a room which had been prepared for him in the Inner Sanctum. It was a single room, as even married couples weren't allowed to share a room in church quarters.

Makes sense, I guess.

It was an understandable enough rule, and not one he was all that opposed to. Life in the Inner Sanctum was the height of simple frugality, and since his room didn't have any candles, the only illumination in the room after the sun went down was the moonlight. Anywhere but the vicinity of the window was pitch dark. It was so dark, Diablo couldn't tell if his eyes were open or not.

"Hmmm…"

His original plan was to regroup with Sylvie and Horn and go straight to Faltra, but then he heard about how the eastern citadel city of Kenstone had fallen to the Gelmed Empire.

One of Lyferia's major cities fell…?

An event like that had never happened in *Cross Reverie*. The Empire of Gelmed was a country that belonged in *Girls' Arms*, anyway. But this wasn't a game, it was a real world, and it wasn't all that weird for a rival country to declare war. So long as Lyferia won, everything would go back to normal. Diablo and his group would have to flee, since they were now wanted, but the capital would be fine.

But what if it loses? Would leaving Lumachina and the capital's residents behind be the right thing to do? Rilitana, the priest who'd helped him, also said that she'd stay in the capital until the war was settled. Horn had her friends from the sorcerer's academy, and Alicia didn't seem to have any plans to leave the capital behind, either.

But I could definitely see Lyferia losing this war...

The life simulation game *Girls' Arms* featured Magimatic Sols. The giant arm and weapon Rose could summon was actually based on that game's setting. In the game, one could use up to twenty Magimatic Sols. The player would customize their equipment and formation, then sortie them out on missions.

The missions' maps usually limited how many units one could deploy, but there was likely no such limitation in this world. At worst, there was the risk of large numbers of Magimatic Sols attacking.

Lyferia had the Palace Knights, who were quite strong, but they likely couldn't match the Magimatic Sols.

Knights from a fantasy setting can't beat robots from a sci-fi setting.

What about Diablo, though? He tried imagining what it would be like to fight Rose... Her mobility was low and all she had were melee weapons, so he could probably manage it. But the Magimatic Sols in *Girls' Arms* could be equipped with long range weapons. The usual formation in that game was to go with half long-ranged units and half-melee units. Thinking about it from *Cross Reverie*'s logic, they were a bad match-up for both elemental sorcerers and magi gunners.

In other words — Diablo had a bad match-up against long-range Magimatic Sols.

"Ugh... That's a fight I don't wanna pick..."

What's worse, Magimatic Sols were manned robots. There were pilots sitting inside them.

I don't know who might be piloting those things, but I don't want to kill anyone.

If he were one to proactively stand up to crisis and trouble, he wouldn't have ended up being a shut-in gamer back in his world. Diablo cut off his contemplations. Brooding over those things was pointless. Instead, his body, which had grown used to a healthy lifestyle, was becoming sleepy with the deepening of the night…

Knock knock!

The sound of a knock at the door jolted him awake. Diablo opened his eyes, seeing a faint light spill in from the window. The sky was growing grey, but it wasn't sunrise yet.

"What's wrong?!" He shouted at the door.

"Diablo!" He heard Rem's voice from behind the door. "The king of Lyferia…!"

"What?!"

Diablo rose from his bed and swung the door open, only to find Rem uncharacteristically panicked.

"The king of Lyferia has died in battle! The army is fleeing!"

"…I see."

He'd predicted something like this might happen, so it didn't come across as much of a shock. Having the king die was one of the worst possible scenarios he'd considered, though.

"What should we do…?!"

"How is the kingdom planning to approach this?"

If the army surrendered, there was no point to them asking to join the fight.

"…The capital's garrisoned forces are preparing a defensive line. There are already many soldiers up on the walls."

"Hmm."

The Inner Sanctum was floating in the sky, and looking out the window, Diablo could see the light of countless torches wavering through the faintly hazy night. There were indeed soldiers stationed on the walls, and if they'd planned to surrender, they'd descend to the ground… which meant they were planning to fight.

"How is the evacuation of the citizens going?" Diablo asked.

"…I don't know," Rem replied.

She was in the same position as him, after all. Just an adventurer from Faltra. She had no way of gaining any detailed information.

Diablo walked away from the window and approached the door.

"First, let's ask Lumachina if she knows anything."

"Yes!"

†

The 《Room of Fire Prayers》, located in the depths of the Inner Sanctum, was filled with a calming aroma. It was from incense, set up to help those in the room stay rational even in this state of emergency. In the center of this large room was a table set with a map of the capital and its surroundings. Tria and the other paladins, who were discussing matters until now, bowed respectfully and left. Diablo and Rem entered as if switching places with them.

Diablo was in his usual outfit by now, but he didn't have his weapon on him, since it was damaged in the previous battle. Rem, on the other hand, was still in men's clothing.

They were fortunate enough to collect Rem and Shera's clothes along with the rest of the carriage, but… Tria had alerted them to the fact that walking around in outfits that displayed navel or cleavage wouldn't be acceptable in the Inner Sanctum. And so, the two remained in those outfits.

"…I'm sorry. Are we interrupting?"

"Not at all, we just finished discussing things," Lumachina answered with a stiff expression.

"…Could you tell us what's going on?"

She nodded, rising from her seat and pointing to the eastern side of the map.

"The Empire's army is approaching us from the east."

"…So they're already coming here."

"It seems they know no rest. A rather reckless campaign, in my opinion…"

"…Is that thanks to their magimatic equipment, too?"

"I don't know. Lyferia's army has fallen back, and the enemy army is in pursuit. The soldiers are trying to enter the capital through the eastern gate."

"…What about evacuating the citizens?"

"All the gates from the sixth to the eleventh district are open." Lumachina pointed to the west side of the map. "Anyone who wishes to flee the capital is allowed to do so… But what will they do? The Gelmed Empire's army is drawing closer. It's hard to imagine any citizens will be able to escape them without anyone to escort them."

"…This is a complicated situation."

There was a high chance the Empire had sent a separate unit to block off the highways, and even Lyferia's army lacked the strength to break through them.

"What will the church do?" Diablo asked.

"I, at the very least, will stay here. I cannot abandon the believers here and flee the capital."

"Hmph… That does sound like something you might do."

The Area Around Caliture City

How *NOT* to Summon a Demon Lord

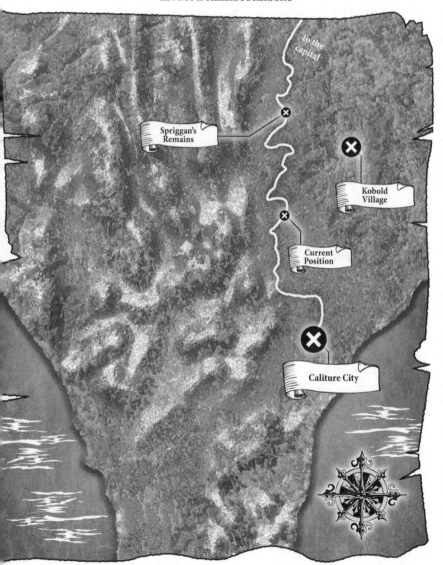

To the capital

Spriggan's
Remains

Kobold
Village

Current
Position

Caliture City

"You're kind as well, Lord Diablo." Lumachina directed her gaze at him. "You've stayed here as well."

Her eyes were full of bottomless trust.

D-Don't look at me like that... Diablo thought in a troubled manner.

He couldn't help thinking that he had to bail, but the only thing holding him back was that "a Demon Lord would never run with his tail between his legs." He hated war, and didn't believe he could protect the capital from the Gelmed army.

"...Diablo will be able to turn this situation around." Rem nodded. "I'm sure of it."

Oh, yikes...

"Hmph... I am a Demon Lord, you fools. I am not one to grant salvation."

So he said, but the girls' gazes didn't change.

"I've already gathered Shera and the others." Lumachina gestured toward the neighboring room.

"Yes." Rem headed toward the door.

Diablo made to follow her, but Lumachina called for him to stop.

"Please, wait."

"Mm?"

"The other day, I received word of an unusual item from the mage's guild..."

"Does it have anything to do with me?"

"I'm not quite sure, but I thought it may be of use to you. And so, I've taken the liberty of having it delivered here."

Lumachina then called out, prompting someone to enter from another room.

†

A familiar girl walked in, dragging a wooden box loaded onto a trolley.

"It's been quite some time. Thank you for helping me back then."

It was a Human girl with sleek black hair, clad in the sorcerer's academy uniform. If he recalled, this was Horn's upperclassman…

"I go by Angeline, I'm a third year from the Sorcerer's Academy's high school wing. I've come here today on behalf of the academy's headmistress to deliver this item to the High Priest."

Whatever was in this box was supposedly related to Diablo. At Lumachina's request, Angeline unlocked the wooden box.

"This item was sold to the capital's mage's guild a short time ago by a certain paladin."

"A paladin?" Diablo tilted his head in confusion.

"He said the High Priest may know of its original owner, and she may return it if she wishes."

She flipped the box's lid open, revealing its contents: a black magic staff. Diablo couldn't believe his eyes.

"Isn't that the 《Tenma's Staff》?!"

Lumachina's expression softened.

"Ah, so it was one of your belongings after all, Lord Diablo!"

Diablo reached out and grabbed hold of the staff. This weight. The clear sensation of magical energy. There was no mistaking it. He had lost this staff when he took Lumachina to the 《Demon Lord's Labyrinth》. It happened when he jumped after Horn, who had fallen into an aqueduct following an attack from Gewalt, the paladin…

"I see. So he picked the staff up and sold it off."

That man would go after the High Priest's life for money, so it made sense he'd snatch the Tenma's Staff, given its high rarity. It was crafty of him, Diablo had to admit, but thanks to that, the staff ended up returning to him.

The Tenma's Staff was an EX rarity magic weapon. Its effects were a significant buff to the wielder's INT stat — which governed magical energy — and reducing the casting time of the wielder's spells. Plain effects, but familiarity was best here. Diablo was very happy to have the weapon he was most familiar with returned to him. A smile naturally crept over his lips.

"Heheh… Ahahaha…"

"E-Erm…" Angeline's expression turned anxious. "Are you sure returning this to him was a good idea…? I'm not being fooled by another evil person again, am I?" she whispered to Lumachina.

"Heheh… Not to worry, you've done the right thing," Lumachina answered with a wry smile.

Rem peeked in from the other room, seemingly curious as to what Diablo was doing.

"Oh, is that…?! Diablo, you got your old staff back!"

"Mmm!"

"…It suits you."

Shera and the others filed into the Room of Fire Prayers.

"Waaah! I haven't seen this thing in so long. You really do look the best with that staff!"

"Heh…"

When Rem and Shera summoned him to this world, he had had the Tenma's Staff equipped, after all. Sylvie and Horn said the same thing, while Alicia and Rilitana hung back. Surely it was okay to get a little excited when girls were complimenting his gear, right?

"Heheheh… The Gelmed Empire is no match for me! I shall obliterate them!" Diablo brandished his staff with grandiosity.

And then:

Boom!

A massive explosion rang out, shaking the Inner Sanctum.

What the hell?!

After a long, tense moment, one of the believers ran into the room, his face as pale as a sheet.

"A-An explosion, an explosion in the castle! The castle is on fire!"

"Diablo?!" Rem and Shera turned tearful looks in Diablo's direction.

"I-It wasn't me!"

†

In the observatory, which sat at the highest level of the Inner Sanctum, they looked down at the castle. It was, indeed, on fire. Crimson flames rose from Castle Grandiose, with black smoke billowing into the air. Alicia leaned into the sight devouringly, her hands pressed against the glass.

"Aah… Aaah…"

Whatever had happened in the past, she was an imperial knight, tasked with defending the kingdom. She must have been quite shocked. She may have wished for mankind's destruction and plotted the Demon Lord's revival at one point in time, but she's since turned over a new leaf…

Wait, did she really?

Diablo stood beside Alicia.

"Pull yourself together, Alicia… Ah?!"

Her expression was ecstatic, and her eyes were positively sparkling. Her mouth was hanging open, and she was almost drooling.

"Haaa… Haaa… Haaa… Aaaah… The castle… it's burning… Haaa… Haaa…"

"Is everything all right?"

"No, no, it most certainly isn't. The Kingdom of Lyferia, it's probably all ov… All o… All over…! ♥"

Her expression didn't match what she was saying.

"No… I mean you, are *you* all right?"

"Huh? Well, let's see? I'm quite anxious… My hands are shaking…"

"Mm."

"My heart is beating quite fast…"

"I see."

"And I simply cannot seem to stop climaxing."

"That sounds fatal. Hey, Rem, have her rest in the back."

Rem nodded with a stiff expression and reached for Alicia's shoulders.

"…I dread to think what might become of you if you watch this any longer, Alicia. Come on, let's rest back here."

"Hihihi… Miss Rem, Miss Shera, look at it! The castle is burning! Has a prettier torch ever been lit?!"

"…Seriously, sit down and rest." Rem dragged her away.

"What's wrong, Alicia?!" Horn also jumped in to help. "You're acting kind of weird. Like, really weird!"

Angeline watched them leave with an anxious expression.

"That woman is… an imperial knight, right…?"

"People have many facets to them," Rilitana said sagely, as if imparting God's teachings.

The words rang rather hollow coming from a priest with a love for nudism, though.

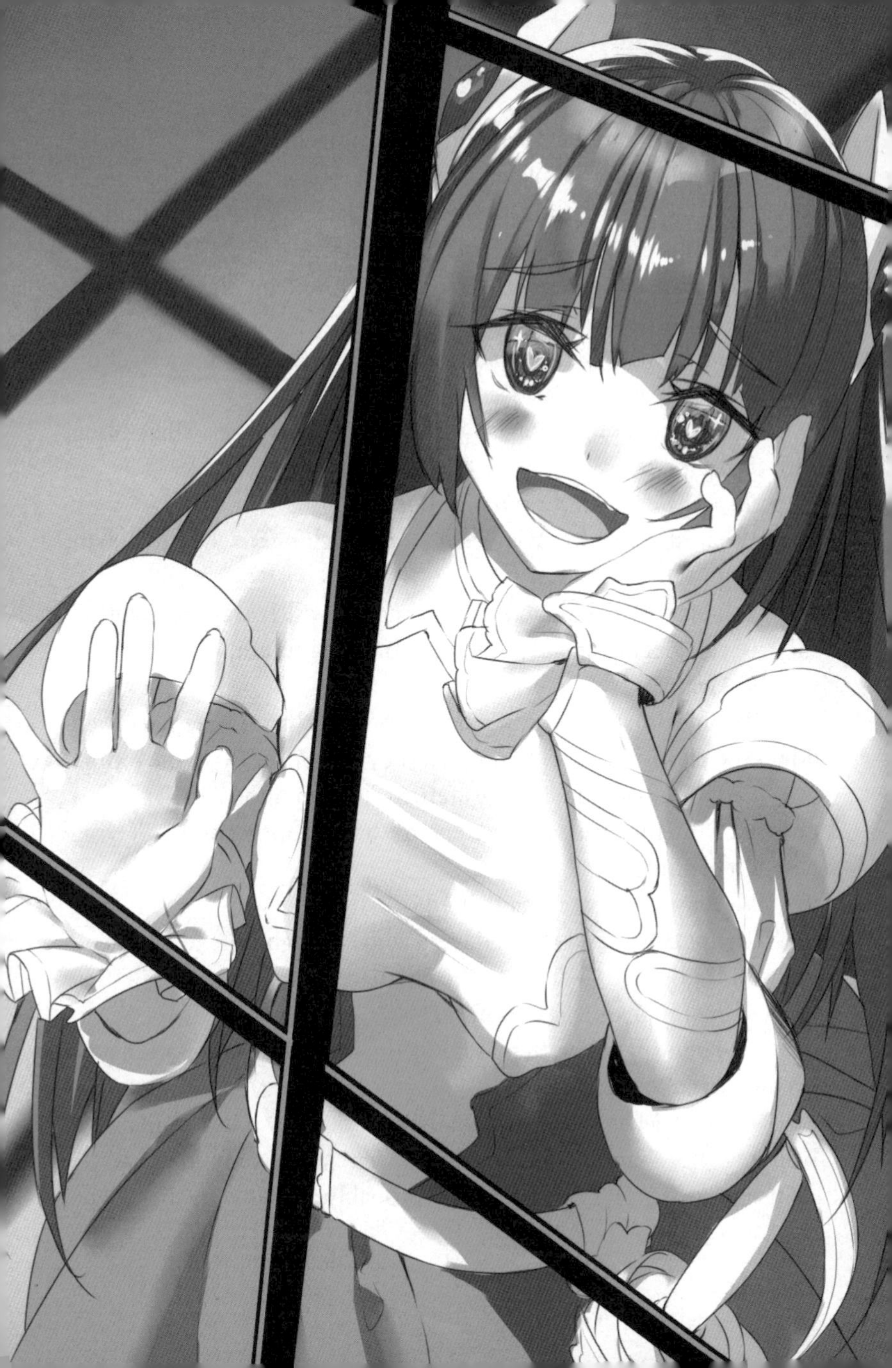

Tria then entered with a report for Lumachina.

"I have a report! Violent conflict has broken out in the castle between a faction wishing to surrender and a faction wanting to fight the Empire!"

"Wait, so… that explosion wasn't caused by the Empire of Gelmed?"

"The surrender faction used summon beasts on the war faction — or so says the report I've been given."

So the people who don't want to fight burned their allies along with the castle.

The kingdom is in terminal condition…

"What do we do, Diablo…?" Shera clung to Diablo's arm, shivering. "I'm scared…"

"You stay with Lumachina. No matter which way the fighting tilts, we can't let anyone approach the Inner Sanctum."

"A-Alright."

Diablo didn't want any part in the war, but if they narrowed down the places they had to protect, they'd have more wiggle room.

"Lady Lumachina, please return to the inner room." Tria nodded. "Intelligence says the enemy has airborne units. Staying here is a liability."

"Very well," Lumachina replied.

"The paladins and the believers who can fight intend to defend the twelfth district. I will go to the northern gate."

"Is the Empire's army coming?"

"The fighting has gotten as far as the third district's eastern gate. It's only a matter of time."

"I see… May good luck shine upon you," Lumachina said, bringing her hands together in prayer. With only that, white light enveloped Tria's body. It was probably invisible to those who couldn't see the flow of magical energy. That was likely the priest class' 《Protection of Light》. It reduced damage inflicted on the target while increasing their attack power. The power of her miracles was, as always, astounding.

I doubt it would be enough against a Magimatic Sol, though.

"I will go as well," Diablo said, tightening his grip on his staff.

"Thank you, Lord Diablo…" Lumachina clasped her hands over her chest. "Please, save us all."

"Do not make me repeat myself. I am simply sweeping away the fools who have invaded my base. I am not doing this to save you."

He only said that to mask his embarrassment, but even he had to admit how silly it sounded this late into the game.

"You have my thanks." Tria bowed her head. "I will deploy the church's soldiers in a defensive line along the twelfth district. Lord Diablo, I ask that you rout the enemy."

She'd judged the situation of the battle on her own and chose to fortify the spots that seemed close to collapse.

"Very well."

"We're counting on you~♪" Sylvie waved at him from the direction of the wall.

"Keep this place safe, understood?"

"Of course."

He didn't intend to let the situation get that far, but… if push came to shove, Lumachina and Shera alone had to escape. The church and the Kingdom of Greenwood, respectively, relied on them. And so Diablo entrusted them to Sylvie, the most reliable person he knew, aside from himself.

Shera had matured a great deal in terms of attack power, and Rem could depend on that suspicious power she used back during their travels in Caliture… But this was a war. They were fighting the races, and the enemies weren't necessarily awful villains.

131

I really don't want to fight, but I don't want them to fight, either...

Diablo clenched his fist. He then heard someone call his name. It was Shera.

"You have to come back..." she said with tears in her eyes. "Definitely, okay?! Definitely, definitely, definitely!"

Diablo felt his lips curl.

"Cease your foolishness, Shera! Remember that I am Diablo, a Demon Lord from another world!" Diablo said, pulling off the bravest Demon Lord role playing he could.

†

He left the Inner Sanctum by using flight magic to soar out one of the windows. Everything was eerily quiet. The capital was uncomfortably large, and the sound of the fighting at the third district's gate was distant. There was no sense of urgency in the air.

"It'd be nice if they just decided to go back home..."

But sadly, his wish didn't reach the heavens. The sound of the battlecries grew closer.

"An attack on the northern gate! It's the Empire's army!"

The enemy attacked just as the sun rose over the horizon. The hostilities had begun. Seven Wall had a Fallen-repelling barrier, but it was meant to repel things that stemmed from magic, such as Fallen, magical beasts, and Demon Lords. It likely had no effect on magimatic equipment, which originated in a whole different setting.

The Gelmed Empire's soldiers attacked with weapons similar to guns, and the Lyferian army met their attacks with magi guns and summon beasts. If the Gelmed Empire's guns operated according to *Girls' Arms* mechanics, they had endless ammo. Arrows, magi guns, and summons, on the other hand, would all eventually deplete. It was just a matter of time.

Should Diablo go out and blast the enemy away with powerful magic?

No. I shouldn't waste my resources here. The enemy I should fight is elsewhere.

Enemies appeared at the northern gate. A white Magimatic Sol! A voice was coming from around its chestpiece, as if magnified by a megaphone.

"Aaah, aaah… Is this thing on? Ahem. People of the Kingdom of Lyferia… This is warrant soldier Rikka Viatona of the Gelmed Empire speaking. I will now engage the kingdom's forces using this Magimatic Sol, Viatanos. If you surrender, we guarantee the safety of both soldiers and civilians."

It was the voice of a young girl.

This really is like Girls' Arms… Diablo thought.

In the game, the heroines came as part of a set along with the robot they piloted, and all of them were cute girls.

"You won't fool us!" a man in a cleric's outfit shouted at her from atop the wall. "The Empire carried my family off and I haven't seen them since!"

The people of the church weren't ones to lose in a war of words, it seemed. Diablo didn't know if it was true, but after hearing that, he doubted anyone would surrender easily.

"Fire!" the commander of the church soldiers ordered with a shout. A volley of arrows and magi gun rounds was fired from the walls toward the white Magimatic Sol, Viatanos.

"Aaaah?!" The Magimatic Sol retreated, holding up a large shield to block the attacks.

Black smoke clouded the large machine. Lyferia's side raised their voice in a cheer… only for their voices to fill with despair once the smoke cleared. The enemy was completely unharmed.

"No way…"

"We can't win against that thing…!"

"*Ugh… Do you get it now? Cease your pointless resistance and surrender!*"

"Then how about you try this on for size…" Diablo said. "《Lightning Storm》!"

It was a level 140 spell that used the light and wind elements. The tornado suppressed the enemy's movements while they were continually zapped by lightning bolts. Diablo launched the spell as he jumped off the walls, eliciting surprised cries from the surrounding believers.

He wasn't in a state of mind to care about what they thought, though. Honestly, if she could shrug off the Lightning Storm, Diablo doubted any of *Cross Reverie*'s attacks could defeat a Magimatic Sol.

"*Gaaaaaaaaaaaah?!*"

Viatanos was blown back and smacked into the ground.

"*Uuu… What was that…?!*"

Its exterior cracked as pieces of its armor chipped off and fell to the ground. Spells did deal damage, it seemed. The church soldiers cheered, but Diablo remained silent.

Daaaamn, it's bulky!

This was a near-maximum-power high level attack spell, and it landed a direct hit, at that. Yet all it did was chip away at its armor. The Magimatic Sol had a magic resistance comparable to that of a Demon Lord. If he was up against one of them with Sasara and Rose acting as a vanguard, he could just blast it away with a powerful spell that required a long incantation.

But Sasara and Rose sadly weren't here, and Diablo couldn't afford to leave the capital when the Empire's army could move in at any time.

And on top of that…

"What are you doing, Rikka?!"

A crimson Magimatic Sol approached them. They were a unit, it seemed. Diablo couldn't tell how many of them there were, but it was more than just one.

"Ah, Erina."

"There are soldiers standing on top of the walls! Just sweep them away!"

"But she might be there, so I can't kill all of them blindly…"

"They're all men, so it's fine! Forget that, if you lose your unit too, we really will…"

"Uuu…"

Diablo didn't know what they meant, but he did realize they were going to attack. This newcomer red Magimatic Sol was equipped with a bulky bow. Diablo glared at this new enemy, when…

Wait, I know this one.

He didn't play Girls' Arms for very long, but this robot belonged to a character that was part of the player's initial unit.

"That's Erina Reufelia's unit… 《Burix of the Red》, if I recall correctly…?"

"Ah?! Why do you… How do you know of me?!"

Diablo was taken aback. Even the character's name was as he remembered. This did nothing to change their relationship, though. This was a battlefield.

Erina steadied her breath.

"Well, I suppose Magimatic Sols are the main force in the Empire army, and I stand head and shoulders above the rest when it comes to operating them. It's no wonder even the enemy knows of me."

"*I dunno about that… It's pretty strange.*"

"*Silence! Even if he is one of my fans, I will stomp him out!*"

Even their exchange was familiar. He'd seen this conversation in-game. Maybe if it wasn't Rem and Shera who summoned them, and he'd have appeared at their side instead… Would he have been their commander?

"*Fall to me!*"

Burix of the Red fired its magimatic bow. It was similar to a magi gun's attack, which meant Diablo's 《Demon Lord's Ring》 couldn't reflect it.

Hasn't this ring been kind of useless lately?!

"《Volcanic Wall》!"

Diablo formed a wall of flames to block the enemy's attack. It lasted through the third shot, but the fourth one cut through.

"Tch…!"

The top of the walls took the attack, and the church soldiers screamed in fright. Diablo descended to the outside of the walls.

I can't let attacks aimed at me harm the soldiers!

Even if he defeated the Magimatic Sols, it would be pointless if the defensive line couldn't hold back the Empire's advance. He couldn't afford to not fight — without him, the church soldiers would be trampled.

So the objective of this quest is to either destroy or push back two Magimatic Sols while the church soldiers can still hang on!

†

More reports reached Lumachina.

The connecting bridge to the first district fell to the Empire's army!

"They've gotten this far already…"

The Empire's army had occupied the first district.

"…I thought the eastern side of the capital was occupied by the remnants of Lyferia's army…" Rem moaned.

"Well, they probably bailed because they saw that they couldn't win." Sylvie shrugged.

Rilitana prepared a relief sector on the lower level of the Inner Sanctum to treat wounded soldiers, and Angeline and Horn joined her to help.

More and more injured soldiers were carried in as the fighting continued. The priests prayed for miracles and healed their wounds, enabling the soldiers to return to full service. The soldiers on the frontlines told each other that "so long as you're not dead, they can patch you up," which greatly supported morale.

"I will go as well," Alicia said, checking her sheathed sword.

She had a dignified expression, as if her odd behavior from earlier was a lie.

"Huh?" Lumachina looked surprised. "Excuse me, Miss Alicia, but… I thought you weren't very skilled in combat."

"Heheh… It is true, my level as a warrior is merely 40."

Relatively speaking, that meant she was quite skilled, but not nearly enough to change the tides of battle.

"It's true that having even one more ally on our side would help. However…"

The Kingdom of Lyferia was in a precarious state, but she still had to keep Alicia's noble position in mind. What's more, Alicia was a woman who was exceedingly useful off the battlefield. When they'd opposed the church, Alicia gathered evidence of the Cardinal Authority's crimes in a very short period of time. And this time, she'd both kept track of Diablo's movements and secured Sylvie and Horn faster than the king's lackeys could capture them.

Those weren't feats just anybody could achieve.

"When we fought the governor of Faltra, I was incapable of helping at all." Alicia smiled thinly. "And when Lady Edelgard was punished by the Fallen, too… I'm well aware of my flaws, but that does not mean I can't change my ways."

"What do you mean?"

"Heheh… Let us just say that might and force come in a variety of forms."

She had something prepared, it seemed.

"Very well." Lumachina nodded. "I wish you the best of luck."

"Thank you very much, Your Eminence."

"…I'll come with you." Rem stepped forward.

"Are you sure?"

"…I'm actually quite strong right now."

Honestly, she knew she couldn't exhibit the massive power she'd wielded when she used the Demon Lord's Fang, but she was still a high level summoner and grappler. She could say with pride that she was a force to be reckoned with.

"Then I'll come along, too!" Shera raised a hand.

"Rejected," Sylvie cut into her words, leaning against the wall with her arms crossed.

"Why?!" Shera grimaced. "I have the bow Klem strengthened for me, I can totally protect everyone!"

"Sorry, but…" Sylvie shook her head. "If anything were to happen to you, Shera, the Kingdom of Greenwood would be done for. If it were just another adventure, it would be one thing, but I can't approve of you standing on the front lines of a war."

"I fought in the war against the Fallen, you know!"

"…That's because we didn't know you had an important role for the Kingdom of Greenwood back then."

"But I'm an adventurer!"

"…Then learn how to keep yourself safe first. Last time I had to use two summons to keep you safe."

"Uuu…"

When they'd fought Gewalt the Palace Knight, Rem used her summons as shields for Shera, who handled offense. This division of roles proved effective, but put another way, it meant Shera couldn't fight without those summons to protect her.

If Rem were alone, she would use all her summons for offense and could use her skills as a grappler, not to mention the Glow, to defend herself.

"Miss Shera, I leave protecting Lady Lumachina to you," Alicia said with a serious voice. "The church's soldiers are on the frontlines, and with Rem and myself joining them, you will be the only one capable of keeping this place safe."

"Huh? Oh… Right."

"I'm only a supportive sorcerer, after all~" Sylvie said with a bitter smile. "I can stall the enemy, but I can't take them out."

"Okay!" Shera nodded. "I'll keep Lumachina safe!"

"I leave it in your capable hands."

Having concluded this matter, Alicia headed for the door. Rem jogged after her, leaving the Room of Fire Prayers behind.

"…Thank you," she said as she walked down the hall alongside Alicia. "Shera's not one to listen to reason once she gets an idea in her head, but this is one time where we can't afford to send her out to fight."

"I would have much preferred it if you stayed behind too, Miss Rem."

"...Do you think I'll get in the way?"

"I believe Lord Diablo would be beside himself with anger toward me if something bad were to befall you."

"...Would he, though?" Rem scratched her cheek.

"Do you wish to test it? Yes, perhaps... if you were to die, Miss Klem would awaken as a true Demon Lord again..." Alicia said with an ecstatic expression.

"...That's a pretty nasty joke," Rem said. "That really hurts, you know?"

Once before, Rem had almost died to the Paladin Saddler due to Alicia's plotting. Assuming she could trust the vision of Klem, or rather the residual presence of the Demon Lord Krebskulm she saw in a dream, Rem had apparently been killed once. She'd crossed a threshold one usually can't go back from, and was only pulled back to life by Shera.

It was a feat of resurrection. Which meant Shera had achieved a miracle surpassing even Lumachina, the High Priest. Rem still had trouble believing it, and hadn't told Diablo about it yet.

"You said you would forgive me, Miss Rem..." Alicia cast down her gaze. "But I think that's a sin I can only pay for with my life."

"...Don't tell me you think now is that time...?"

"I've no intention of dying in vain."

Which means she is willing to die if it isn't in vain, Rem thought. She then changed the conversation's direction.

"...Alicia, please hear me out. The king of Lyferia has passed away. I don't know how many of the influential nobles and staff officers remain, but most of the military they held power over has died, as well. The very structure of the Kingdom of Lyferia has collapsed."

"…Are you trying to bring me to orgasm?"

"No! I'm saying that if you hate the kingdom's corruption so much, this is your chance to create a country without that corruption!"

"A country…"

"…It will be difficult to push back the Empire of Gelmed given the state of this war… But if we can manage that, we will have to rebuild the country after the war. And when that happens, we'll need people like you. You have the bloodline and status of the old regime, decisiveness and leadership skills, and you know how to shift manpower and resources. Most of all, you have a heart that hates injustice."

And you're good at scheming, Rem thought, but kept those words unsaid.

"You say the oddest things, Miss Rem…" Alicia said with a sad smile. "I'm a Demon Lord worshiper, remember?"

"…Even now?"

"I worship Lord Diablo now."

"…He does claim to be a Demon Lord, I suppose." Rem crossed her arms with a moan.

"Does Lord Diablo… really wish for this country's restoration?" Alicia asked curiously. "Wouldn't he wish to see everything burn to the ground?"

"…I don't think he'd be out fighting to protect people right now if he really thought that."

"I thought he was only doing that for Lady Lumachina."

"…Diablo can say all sorts of things, but he cherishes peace, appreciates the lives of others, and hates wrongdoing."

"You make him sound like… a hero."

"…That is how I think of him." Rem didn't deny it.

"The restoration of this country, you say…" Alicia said with a faraway look in her eyes.

"…I think that's when your power will be needed most."

"Heheh… I do think you're overselling me, but if Lord Diablo wishes for it, I would devote all that I have for that purpose."

"…Then once this fight is over, you should ask him," Rem said.

Though she had to anxiously hope she would ask him in a way that wouldn't cause any misunderstandings.

Rem and Alicia finally exited the Inner Sanctum only for an explosion to deafen their ears and a shockwave to wash over them. The smell of something burning tickled at their nostrils, and the sounds of swords, gunshots, and screams could be heard.

It was a battlefield.

"Let us go, Miss Rem!" Alicia burst into a run. "We must defend the connecting bridge!"

"Yes!"

Rem clenched a summon crystal tightly in her hands.

"《Cross Blizzard》!" Diablo unleashed his spell.

It was a level 110 water and air elemental spell. It formed two tornados that froze anything they touched, then shattering them with raging winds. The Gelmed Empire's soldiers screamed as they ran for safety.

"Retreat! Retreat!"

They were equipped with magimatic gear, but they couldn't tank spells of this level. Some of the soldiers couldn't escape in time, becoming statues of ice and breaking into pieces.

"Ugh…"

Diablo's heart creaked. The Gelmed soldiers were the enemy. They killed many of Lyferia's and the church's soldiers, and even some civilians. Diablo didn't have the leisure of caring for the lives of his foes right now.

But the Magimatic Sols moved even with the Cross Blizzard's effects.

"Fall back! All ordinary soldiers, fall back!" the red unit cried out.

"Whoaa…" the white unit said in amazement. *"Everything looks white!"*

The pilots didn't seem awfully burdened by the spell.

"Did my unit's eyes freeze over?! I can't see anything! Rikka, are you all right?! Rikka!"

"Erina, calm down. Just use your unit's heat rays."

143

"*Ah… Right you are.*"

The Magimatic Sols' heads had frozen over, but soon returned to normal. Their armor was slightly cracked. Diablo's spells were affecting them, but it was only chipping away at them. They then launched their counterattacks.

"*Fall! Fall! I am ordering you to fall!*"

"*You're not hitting him…*"

"*You shoot him too, Rikka!*"

"*But my rig's a melee-combat type…*"

Viatanos of the White was holding a shield, which apparently counted as its weapon. Diablo fought from a distance, so the enemy's only way of hitting him was Burix of the Red's magimatic bow. Its shots were accurate, but predictable. The Magimatic Sol's specs were absurd, but its pilot's skills were mediocre.

Thanks to that, Diablo could hold an even fight despite the odds being against him.

This is bad.

Since the Empire was based off of Girls' Arms, Diablo doubted there were only two Magimatic Sols. There were probably others deployed on other battlefields. Diablo's limit-broken gear was only barely putting a dent in the enemy, and Lyferia's ordinary soldiers were being stomped out like bugs. He didn't have the time to dawdle here.

"Shit… But still…" Diablo clenched his teeth.

"*Why can't I hit him?!*" The two Magimatic Sols seemed to be quarreling. "*Is my magimatic bow broken or something?!*"

"*Maybe you're just a bad shot, Erina.*"

"*Excuse you?! I'll remember what you just said, Rikka!*"

"*Aaaah…*"

Diablo fell into bitter silence. The combat plan he had worked out in his head fizzled out.

They were kids. The Magimatic Sols were powerful, and they had likely killed many soldiers with them, so he couldn't claim they were innocent children.

But still, I don't want to have to kill them...

This may be a war, but he couldn't just kill his enemies the same way he would slay a monster...

†

"Die." Alicia threw a magic stone.

The stone fell at the Gelmed soldiers' feet and... exploded!

In terms of effect, it was equivalent to a 《Flare Burst》 spell, packing enough power to blow away a large Fallen. The Gelmed soldiers were equipped with magimatic shields, but the blast easily penetrated their magical defenses. The soldiers were blown apart, becoming chunks of meat.

"...A-Amazing..." Rem said, her eyes wide with shock.

Alicia removed a few more stones from a pouch on her waist.

"Should I try a water element one next?"

"Fall back! Retreat, retreat!" The Gelmed soldiers began fleeing.

"My... What a shame."

The thousand-or-so soldiers who were pushing into the connecting bridge fell back to the twelfth district. The defending church soldiers started to cheer.

"That was great, Alicia!" Rem praised her.

"Thank you kindly, Miss Rem."

"...What are those things?"

"Fundamentally, they're not much different from magi gun bullets. They have high-level magic sealed in them, all it takes is a bit of magical energy to unleash it."

"These stones can do that?! Then we can use these to beat the Empire's army! Forget that — with these, even a common citizen can beat the Fallen, or even the Demon Lord!"

"Assuming one can gather enough of them."

"…Would that be difficult?"

"They were only developed because the Cristela family requested that the capital's Mage's Guild research them… But there are still some problems."

"…Like what?"

"These magic stones…" Alicia smiled bitterly. "They're worth more than a lump of gold of the same weight."

"Huh?!" Rem flinched, eyeing these magic stones that were certainly larger than a hen's egg.

One of these was likely worth more than all the money Rem earned adventuring last year.

"Creating them consumes a great deal of precious metals." Alicia shrugged.

And so, they cost an absurd fortune to produce. And it wasn't something one could simply order with money — precious metals weren't exactly easy to find.

"…Don't tell me… you only have a few left?" Rem asked anxiously.

"I should very much hope the Empire gives up soon."

But things were sadly not quite that simple. The connecting bridge wavered under the clamoring of heavy, approaching footsteps. A figure rose from behind a building — the hulking figure of a massive suit of armor. It was a purple-colored Magimatic Sol, named Violanos.

"People of Lyferia! You'll find that I'm not as kind as Aira!"

Its pilot was Corporal Migurtha, and it was carrying a massive rifle. Its shape was more angular compared to the ones used by Lyferia's army. Its muzzle was fixed their way. Filled with a sense of dread, Rem quickly called for her summons.

"Come forth, ⟪Iron Golem⟫ and ⟪Iron Gorilla⟫!"

Two massive forms appeared before them, and at the same time, Violanos fired its magimatic rifle in a rapid-fire burst. The bullets moved faster than the speed of sound, impacting the summons and distorting their forms. Becoming riddled with holes in an instant, they crumbled back into black crystals which returned to Rem's hands.

"No!"

They couldn't even serve as shields, and could barely buy Rem and Alicia the time to hide between buildings. Still, Rem was thankful for the summon beasts. If she hadn't used them, Rem and Alicia would have been blown to bits.

The church soldiers seemed to have suffered considerable losses, however. Moans and cries for help could be heard in every direction.

†

"Kuh…" Rem clenched her teeth.

The purple Magimatic Sol only attacked them once! Only once, and that alone left the formation that was defending the connecting bridge completely in tatters. Peering at the enemy from the shadow of a building, Rem noticed something droop into her field of vision.

A lock of orange hair... her wig.

She was still dressed as a man, come to think of it. The shockwaves of this attack must have knocked a hairpin off. She'd kept to this outfit since her usual one wasn't fitting in the Inner Sanctum, but... this wasn't the Inner Sanctum, and this wasn't peacetime, either.

"...Enough already."

Rem tore off the orange-colored wig, which was the color of a typical Pantherian's hair, and spread out her natural long, black hair. She then tore off her tight jacket and returned to her usual, mobile outfit.

"I think you look better this way, Miss Rem." Alicia cracked a smile as she looked at her from the side.

"...I feel the same way. Though I didn't much like the way I looked up until recently."

"A change of heart?"

"...There's someone who acknowledges me now," Rem said, dropping her gaze to her ring finger.

The wedding ring sparkled, as if to meet her gaze.

"I think that's lovely." Alicia nodded.

"...We haven't done anything a married couple usually does, though."

"Yes, that man is simply like that, it seems."

"...And that's why I can't afford to die here."

"Indeed."

They turned their attention back to the battle at hand. The church soldiers launched sporadic attacks, but... in line with the intelligence they received, conventional weapons couldn't affect Magimatic Sols.

The purple Magimatic Sol, Violanos, stepped onto the connecting bridge.

"Stop hiding and come on out! I'll pump you full of holes!"

She fired again in their direction, and if it weren't for the stone walls they hid behind, she'd likely have shot them through. The buildings jolted as the blasting sounds of her shots rocked the air. Her barrage was horrifying.

"…I'll draw in her attacks."

"Miss Rem?!"

"…Your magic stones might deal some damage."

They were as powerful as Diablo's spells. If the stones had no effect, then they really were out of options. Alicia thought the same thing and didn't deny it.

"But you can throw these stones just the same as I can, Miss Rem. I'll leave them all to you, so let me handle the role of bait."

"…Me playing bait doesn't mean I intend to die. I'm different now from how I was before. Stronger than when Diablo always had to protect me."

"I… see."

"…But I can't keep it up for very long, so please."

"Understood. Leave it to me, Miss Rem!"

"I'm off!"

Rem jumped out from their hiding place.

"Come forth, 《Asulau》!" she called out and threw a crystal.

A massive bull with three horns appeared from thin air and fiercely charged the enemy.

"You think this can stop me? What a bad joke."

"You too, 《Rockpup》 and 《Dragonfly》!"

"Small fry! Irritating small fry!"

Violanos fired its rifle again, and the summon beasts were finished within moments. No good after all. She was confident she had matured as a sorcerer, but the beasts she had contracted were of low level.

And so, Rem used the Glow.

Everything accelerated.

Slow, too slow! I ran faster back then! I may have used the Demon Lord's Fang when I fought Gewalt, but that was still my power! I should be able to use it again!

"Concentrate, Rem. Push away all unnecessary thoughts and face your own body."

A memory of her late father's voice surfaced in her mind. And the next moment...

She could see a bullet rushing toward her. If it hit her, she'd die. Rem instinctively weaved the Glow in her fingertips and pressed them against the bullet from the side, pushing away its destructive damage.

Her fingers creaked with a crunching sound. Her skin tore, and then... *ping!* A metallic sound rang out and the bullet deviated from Rem.

"*What?!*" Migurtha's eyes widened with shock. "*That should have been a perfect hit!*"

Rem swiftly ran for cover behind another building. Her heart was beating wildly like a drum.

Did I just... instinctively do something really amazing?!

She didn't feel like she could pull it off again. She was only lucky this time, and she'd eventually need to turn this coincidence into actual skill, but right now she was critically lacking in training. She could tell that much.

"Fighting... like this, based on just talent, doesn't suit me," she muttered in a shaking voice. "I'll leave that to Shera."

The building she was hiding behind was being peppered by Violanos' shots. Rem would need to stall the enemy a bit longer for Alicia to throw her magic stones. But just as Rem started thinking about what to do next, the situation suddenly changed.

†

Clouds gathered in the sky. The sunlight was blotted out and the area around them turned dark.

"What..?"

The black clouds swirling in the sky contorted, forming the outlines of an old man's face. His eyes' fundi were sunken in, and his wrinkled skin was covered in cracks. The man parted his lips, revealing a mouth lacking a few teeth, and spoke in a hoarse voice. *"It is her! There can be no mistaking it! The Girl of the Vessel is before my eyes! Guh, aah, gah!"*

The old man began coughing up blood and the image in the sky contorted and changed again, taking on the shape of…

"…Huh? Isn't that me?"

It was an image of Rem that appeared as if it was looking down on her. She felt an alarming intent directed on her from the Gelmed army, as if a thousand gazes fixed on her at once. Heavy footsteps were approaching her.

Peeking out from behind the building, Rem saw ⟪Violanos of the Purple⟫ cross the connecting bridge composedly.

"Oh, so it was you… It was you! Do you have any idea how many people were taken away because of you… Because you were here…?!" Migurtha raised her voice in a cry that seemed to bellow up from the depths of the earth.

What is she talking about…?

Rem couldn't understand, and honestly, couldn't care less about Migurtha's circumstances. The only thing she understood was that right now, she had just become the Gelmed Empire's target. Her heart was filled with terror, but it did make her perfect for diverting the enemy's attention.

To her surprise, Violanos cast away its rifle. Was it out of bullets? No... Rem recalled what the old man said earlier.

Is she trying to take me alive?

Capturing her alive was much harder than killing her. In that regard, the situation was in Rem's favor.

Or so she thought, but the sounds of the fighting grew that much louder around her. The Empire soldiers, who had kept their distance until now, were rushing around her.

"Go, go, go! That's her! Capture the Girl of the Vessel!"

The church soldiers rose up with weapons in hand.

"Don't let them get any closer! Fight back!"

Rem could tell — all the Gelmed soldiers here were after her. A shiver ran down her spine. Violanos kicked the ground with a thud, rushing toward her rapidly. Rem was surprised at its agility; it broke through the church soldiers' line of defense, rushing to where Rem was hiding. Within a moment, the Magimatic Sol stood before her eyes.

"You are never getting away!"

"Kuh...?!"

Rem had no reason to stick around and be caught by the armored hand. She broke into a run.

"I said you're not getting away!"

But as Violanos was about to take off after her, a flashy explosion rocked Violanos' back. Its purple armor crumbled.

"Kyaaaaaaaah?!"

In contrast to her menacing voice from earlier, this scream was almost adorable. Violanos staggered, leaning against a wall to stay on its feet… But then some more magic stones were tossed at her. This time the ground bulged up, sending the Magimatic Sol flying into the air like a child's toy.

"Aaaaaaaaaaaaaaaaaah?!"

It was Alicia. She had thrown the magic stones while hiding behind one of the buildings.

"Miss Rem, you must run!"

"…Yes!" Rem replied after a moment's hesitation.

The situation had changed. Their objective — defeat the Magimatic Sol and defend the bridge — hadn't changed, but right now, Rem was the target of every single soldier in the Gelmed Empire.

I have to focus on surviving!

Up in the sky, the image of Rem running through the city was reflected in the clouds. She was being watched, and it meant that she couldn't simply hide or escape the capital in secret.

What do I do?!

She could hear heavy footsteps rumble ahead of her. Had Violanos cut her off? No. A white Magimatic Sol carrying a shield appeared, knocking down the wayside trees as it rushed toward her.

"There she is! Found her!" the pilot exclaimed with a childish voice.

†

Diablo looked up into the sky, where an old man's face appeared and started shouting something. He didn't care much about that. But when he saw what appeared in the sky next...

"Rem?!"

The two Magimatic Sols he was up against stirred.

"Rikka, go after the Girl of the Vessel! I can handle this spot alone!"

"Alright! Be careful, Erina!"

Viatanos of the White took off into the city. Jumping over the walls was child's play for a Magimatic Sol. Diablo tried using his magic to stop it, but the magimatic bow fired a barrage to disturb his chanting.

"I will be your opponent!"

"Do not get in my way!"

"I should take those words and throw them right back at you!"

The rumbling of a massive explosion reached Diablo's ears. It seemed to have come from the direction of the connecting bridge to the twelfth district. A pillar of flames rose from there. Diablo didn't have any information about what was going on, but whoever was fighting there must have been extraordinary. Diablo noticed a flash of red hair from the image of Rem in the sky.

Alicia?!

Diablo doubted she could help in any way against a Magimatic Sol. Meanwhile, Rem was running away, only to soon be discovered by Viatanos of the White. From the Gelmed Empire's perspective, everything was going as planned. Burix of the Red opposed Diablo, but didn't attempt any risky attacks. Erina knew that regardless of whether she defeated Diablo, the Girl of the Vessel would be captured sooner or later, and they'd be able to break into the church from another direction at some point, too.

Diablo lowered his staff silently.

"My, throwing in the towel? Did you realize that there's no winning against the Empire?" Erina asked in a sympathetic tone.

She didn't take advantage of this moment to attack, either. These pilots, they… they weren't bad people.

—But he still had to kill them.

"I've been… wrong."

Somewhere in his heart, he'd always been running away from battle. He didn't want to fight the races. There was nothing he wanted less than war. He figured that after a bit of fighting, it would just end on its own.

He feared becoming a murderer.

He could only enjoy *playing the part of* a diabolical, heinous villain in the game, because that was all it was. A game. No one really died there.

I never really wanted to become an actual villain…! But because of my naivete, Rem is…!

The white Magimatic Sol was drawing in on her.

Diablo didn't want to kill. Breaking that ethical taboo pained his conscience.

He was scared.

He wanted to always be a good, upstanding person, but staying that way meant he couldn't protect the person that mattered to him!

Diablo clenched his fingers hard around the staff. He reached into his pouch and took out three potion tubes, downing them immediately. An MP potion, an HP potion, and a buffing potion! Diablo felt his blood seethe. Behind the elation of his battle lust, his thoughts were as cold as ice, and everything disappeared besides the battle before his eyes.

"You still intend to fight?" Erina asked suspiciously, noticing the change in Diablo's behavior. *"I'll have you know that you will never beat me!"*

"This happened before."

"What?"

"Whenever I saw a couple... making out before my eyes... Everything stopped mattering. All the pointless thoughts disappeared, and I could focus on fighting and nothing else."

"Th-That sounds like envy."

"Maybe? But this, right now... This is different. I'm different. I've been wrong this whole time."

"...Y-You..."

Diablo held up his staff.

"I... of my own will... for my own sake, I will kill. I will kill you, and with maximum efficiency!"

"That's obvious! This is a battlefield, after all!" Erina fired a bullet at him.

Diablo evaded and unleashed a spell.

"《Lightning Arrow》!"

Several bullets of shining light left his staff. It wasn't a spell with much firepower behind it, and even if it did hit the Magimatic Sol, all it would do was scorch the armor. But instead, it hit the Gelmed Empire's standard soldiers. Even with magimatic gear, they couldn't block Diablo's attacks.

Numerous screams pierced the air, and Burix of the Red raised its voice in shock.

"Everyone, what's...? What is the meaning of this, sorcerer...?!"

Her attention switched to the soldiers for a moment. And that was all Diablo needed. He used the rushing martial art 《Sword Smite III》, closing the distance between them in the blink of an eye.

"Whenever you fire a stray shot, you look away for a moment. Since you're safe behind your thick armor, your grasp on the basics is faulty!"

"*What?!*"

Burix used its magimatic bow like a sword, swiping horizontally at Diablo. But before it could connect, Diablo touched the head of the Magimatic Sol.

"《Light》!"

"*Hiyaaa?! What?! What is this?!*"

It was nothing but an illumination spell that produced a source of light, but he cast it directly into the Magimatic Sol's eyes — into the lenses of the robot's cameras, filling its field of vision with white.

He wasn't fighting it this long for no reason. He was studying the Magimatic Sol's structure and limits.

"You can't fight if you can't see the enemy."

"*I can still fight!*"

The crimson Magimatic Sol opened its chest piece. The one riding inside was a child that looked strikingly similar to the character that piloted it in *Girls' Arms*. A determined, dignified girl, who'd sometimes turn teary-eyed whenever she made a clumsy mistake:

Erina Reufelia.

She was mostly naked, and buried within a mass of writhing, disgusting tentacles. Facing her directly made him waver, but Diablo suppressed all his doubts.

"You're a fool to expose yourself to me! Flare Burst!"

"Kuuuu!"

If the spell were to hit the open parts of the armor, its power wouldn't be mitigated by the Magimatic Sol's high magic defense. She shielded herself by holding up the unit's right arm, since her left was equipped with the magimatic bow.

Diablo had read her perfectly, down to the way she blocked the attack. A pang of pain crossed Diablo's heart, but… he couldn't afford to be stalled here any longer.

"It's over."

"Huh?" Erina said with a suspicious expression, apparently not understanding what he meant.

The hand she had shielded herself with — the Magimatic Sol's right hand, was lighting up with magical energy.

"…It can't be."

When Diablo touched her, he'd cast a Light spell at the unit's eyes. And immediately after, he cast another spell. The unit's right hand was held up before the opened chestpiece. And from within it, the spell he had set was triggered — aiming at the pilot.

"It's a 《Burst Mine》. It explodes on contact… Or after a set period of time."

Magical flames impacted Burix of the Red from the inside.

"No…!"

Her final words were cut off by the sound of the explosion. Tentacles scattered into the air, and the bulky Magimatic Sol spurted flames from the gaps of its thick armor, before collapsing powerlessly.

The soldiers on both sides of the conflict shuddered. Diablo felt his breath clog in his throat as he gazed into the cockpit of the still Magimatic Sol.

But he couldn't stay put. He turned around and sprinted toward the city.

Please be safe, Rem…!

†

Rem was cornered against a wall. Viatanos of the White wasn't simply sturdy, but also moved with a speed one would never imagine from its size. It swung its massive hands over Rem's head.

Rem dodged, but to her surprise, the Magimatic Sol had foreseen where she'd evade to. The hand changed its trajectory in the last second.

"Gaaaaah?!"

An impact ran through Rem's left leg, followed by a burning sensation. Her leg felt like it was on fire — heat. Seething, agonizing heat. This heat became pain.

Viatanos' hand had crushed Rem's left leg, reducing it to a lump of flesh without a trace of its original shape.

"Aaah… Aaaaaaaah…"

Now wasn't the time to cry, but Rem couldn't hold back the tears welling up in her eyes.

"Alright, I got her!" cheered the voice of Viatanos of the White — Rikka's voice.

Her tone was innocent, as if she were a child who had just caught a bug.

"Uugh, aaah, aaaaaah…!" Rem screamed.

The remains of her left leg seared as if it had just been dipped in fire. The pain was so intense she couldn't even breathe properly, but she still had to run. Rem crawled away, using both arms and her remaining right leg to push her body forward.

"Huh? Guess I should break her other leg, too… There!"

"Aaaaaaaaaaaaaaaaaaaaaaaaaaaaaaaaah?!"

Her body felt like it had been sewn to the ground. Unable to move, both of her legs now wailed in agony. She felt like a piece of wood tossed into a campfire. The rest of her body began growing cold in spite of this sensation — her temperature was dropping due to the volume of blood she was losing. The chill was so intense that Rem's teeth started chattering, her hands shivering. Her body refused to budge, but she couldn't stop twitching. And as Rem lay still, Viatanos looked down on her.

"Aaah, aaah… Aira, do you read? I've caught the Girl of the Vessel. Can you call someone to carry her away? I'm not good with carrying people."

Another Magimatic Sol in purple armor soon approached them. Violanos… Its left arm was missing, but that was all.

"Did you catch her, Rikka?!"

"Yes! I really worked hard for it, too! Wait, Migurtha, are you all right?!"

"I'm fine."

"Whoooooa… I can't believe a Magimatic Sol had its arm blown off like that… Who did this to you?"

"Must have been some kind of sorcerer… I don't really know, but I knocked her away. I haven't checked if she actually died, though."

"Weird."

"She was surrounded by soldiers, so I left her to them."

"I see!"

"Forget that, we have to be cautious. Since our soldiers are gathering here, the kingdom's soldiers are also starting to close in on this place."

"Okay!"

Rikka looked up at the sky. Even now, the Girl of the Vessel was being reflected there by some unknown means. And so was the image of Rikka — or rather, Viatanos of the White — looking up. It was a gruesome sight.

The image didn't transmit any sound, but any kingdom soldier… No, maybe even some of the Empire's soldiers might feel inclined to come to the girl's rescue at the sight of this.

Rikka sighed.

"I mean, it's our mission, but… Mm?"

She turned her gaze to where something caught her attention. Someone was approaching from atop one of the buildings — a man clad in black and wielding a staff, a Demon with horns growing out of his head.

"…Isn't that the sorcerer Erina was taking care of…?! Wait, what happened to Erina?!"

"What's wrong?!" Migurtha asked her urgently.

"No way! Erina can't be… It can't be!"

Rikka glared at the black sorcerer. He was holding a massive black bow and arrow.

†

Diablo began chanting his second multiplex spell.

"Void that swallows all of creation, come to me… 《Black Hole Arrow》!"

Skipping all introductions, he fired such a powerful spell at them right off the bat. It was admittedly not very Demon Lord-ly of him. If he had to fight, he should fight them head on with dignity, but right now, he cast aside those particularities. He didn't care how lame it would make him look. There were two Magimatic Sols. If he took the time to introduce himself, one of them might carry Rem off while he was fighting the other. They wouldn't just leave her there like a prize for the winner to take.

This was a battlefield, and it was only natural the enemy would act the way they did. If he were to rest on his laurels and lose Rem over that, he would never be able to forgive himself!

"Arrow of the void, pierce through and wedge between the boundary of heaven and earth! 《Gravity Abyss》!"

The arrowhead shined with a black glow as it soared toward the Magimatic Sol. The air positively shivered at this crystallization of two massive spells.

"What...?!"

The Magimatic Sol was quick, but it couldn't evade the arrow. Its frame was simply too large. The enemy held up their massive shield, blocking the attack, but the spell triggered nonetheless, creating a black hole that began dragging the shield into it.

The stalwart armor that had withstood multiple spells from Diablo was now squashed far too easily.

"Aaaah! Aaaah! Aaaah! What?! What is this?!"

A hole the diameter of a baseball began dragging everything around it into its confines. Realizing something was wrong, Migurtha raised her voice roughly.

"What's wrong, Rikka?!"

"I don't know! M-My shield... it's being crushed...!"

"Hurry, you must purge it!"

This world isn't inside a game. Being dragged into a Gravity Abyss spell meant certain death. There were no resets. There was no game over screen, after which one could switch off the computer, go take a piss, hit the sack, and try again the next day. Death meant death. As simple as that. And in this kind of world...

"I will... use magic against other people. I will kill my enemies, and save Rem...! 《Lightning Meteor》!"

Lightning struck down from above, holding the newly arrived purple Magimatic Sol in check.

"Kuh… Another sorcerer?!" The purple Magimatic Sol jumped away.

Using this chance, Diablo sprinted forward. He ran and ran, reaching Rem's side.

"Rem!" He kneeled beside her.

Her eyes, moist with tears, opened wide. He could see her mouth his name, but no voice escaped her throat. He wanted to use a potion right now, but he didn't have the time for it. Violanos of the Purple was rushing toward him.

"We can't let you have her! No matter what!"

"My thoughts exactly. No matter what, I won't let you take her away. 《Prism Wall》!"

A rainbow-colored wall spread out before him. It was a magical barrier containing the power of the four great elements — water, earth, air, and fire — as well as light and darkness. It took a moment for it to form, but it would stay up, no matter what, for ten or so seconds after forming. Even if a Magimatic Sol were to ram it at full force, the Prism Wall would take it.

"What in the world is this?!"

While the enemy was bewildered, Diablo picked Rem up.

"Let's go."

Rem simply nodded back wearily. Her legs were terribly crushed, filling Diablo with guilt at being late.

I should have been more decisive.

He used flight magic to quickly soar away. Meanwhile, the Gravity Abyss reached the point where its effect was strongest.

"Migurtha! Migurtha! Help! Please, save me!"

"Huh, this can't be… Rikka… You…?!"

Viatanos of the White's left half was already consumed by the black hole, the pilot half-crushed. Despite its small size, its gravity well was sucking everything in. No matter how thick and sturdy the Magimatic Sol's armor could have been, it wouldn't have made a difference. Its shell bent out of shape, crumbled into pieces, and vanished into the well.

"Aaah, aaaaaaaaah... Nooo! It's crushing me! It's tearing me apart! Save meeee! Migurtha, Migurthaaaa! Airaaaaaaaa! Somebody, save meeeeeeeee!"

"Discard your unit, Rikka!"

"It won't budge! It won't open, it won't... Aaaaaaaah... Mommy, big sister... Save me... Somebody, please save meeeeeeeeeeee!"

And with her final scream, the white Magimatic Sol disappeared into the gravity well. It happened roughly at the same time the Prism Wall's effect died down. Violanos rushed over to where Rikka had been, finding there was no one and nothing left, and froze in place.

"Fall back, Migurtha..." Aira's voice reached her ears, mixed in with static noise. *"We've conquered the castle. The operation is complete."*

"...What are you saying? Rikka is... She's gone..."

"We've lost contact with Erina, too."

"No... But the two of them... They were so lively this morning, I..."

"I know."

"I'll kill him... That sorcerer, I'll kill him...!"

"You will. But you need to get your unit fixed first, Migurtha."

"Why?! The Girl of the Vessel was right there...!"

"This isn't an opponent you can fight without a weapon! Do you want me to lose you, too?!"

"Ugh..."

"Come back, Migurtha."

"Kh... Uuu... Aaah... Aira... Aaaaaaaaaaaaaaaaaaaaaaaaaaaaaah!"

†

Diablo laid Rem down on the ground.

"You're alive, right?"

Rem said nothing. Even parting her lips was too much right now. She looked at him with hollow eyes and barely managed to jerk a nod. Both her legs were completely crushed. Diablo etched that image into his heart, never to forget it for as long as he lived. This was the moment his own naivete had nearly cost Rem her life.

Diablo took out a high-rarity HP recovery potion and propped Rem up, tipping its contents into her mouth. And then, like a film being rewound, her crushed legs rapidly regained their original shape.

At some point, the projection in the sky disappeared. Whatever was keeping an eye on Rem had left. Was it some kind of drone? Diablo would need to think of a countermeasure. Meanwhile, Rem coughed a few times, and then spoke, her voice still weakened.

"…Thank you, Diablo."

"No, I was late. Forgive me."

"…No, I was overconfident because of last time. I was stupid. As dumb as a bag of hammers."

"So was I."

"…As dumb as a bag of hammers?"

"Y-Yes."

But the reality was nothing as cute as that. Diablo knew he could never forget this moment.

I've taken other people's lives, for my own sake.

They were enemies, true, but they were opponents he could talk to. They cared for their comrades and fought for the sake of others. Diablo's heart creaked. He clenched his shaking fist, only to feel a small hand rest over it. Rem's hand.

"…I'm sorry. You did this because of me."

"Don't be stupid. They were the Empire's people. They came to invade us."

"…If you're feeling guilty over this, let me carry half that weight. After all, you and I are…"

"Rem…"

She closed her eyes.

And for some odd reason, Diablo didn't feel any bashfulness or doubts. The desire to confirm that he'd really saved her, as well as the fear that he might never touch her again tomorrow, brushed all those anxieties aside.

Diablo leaned his face in, and the two locked lips.

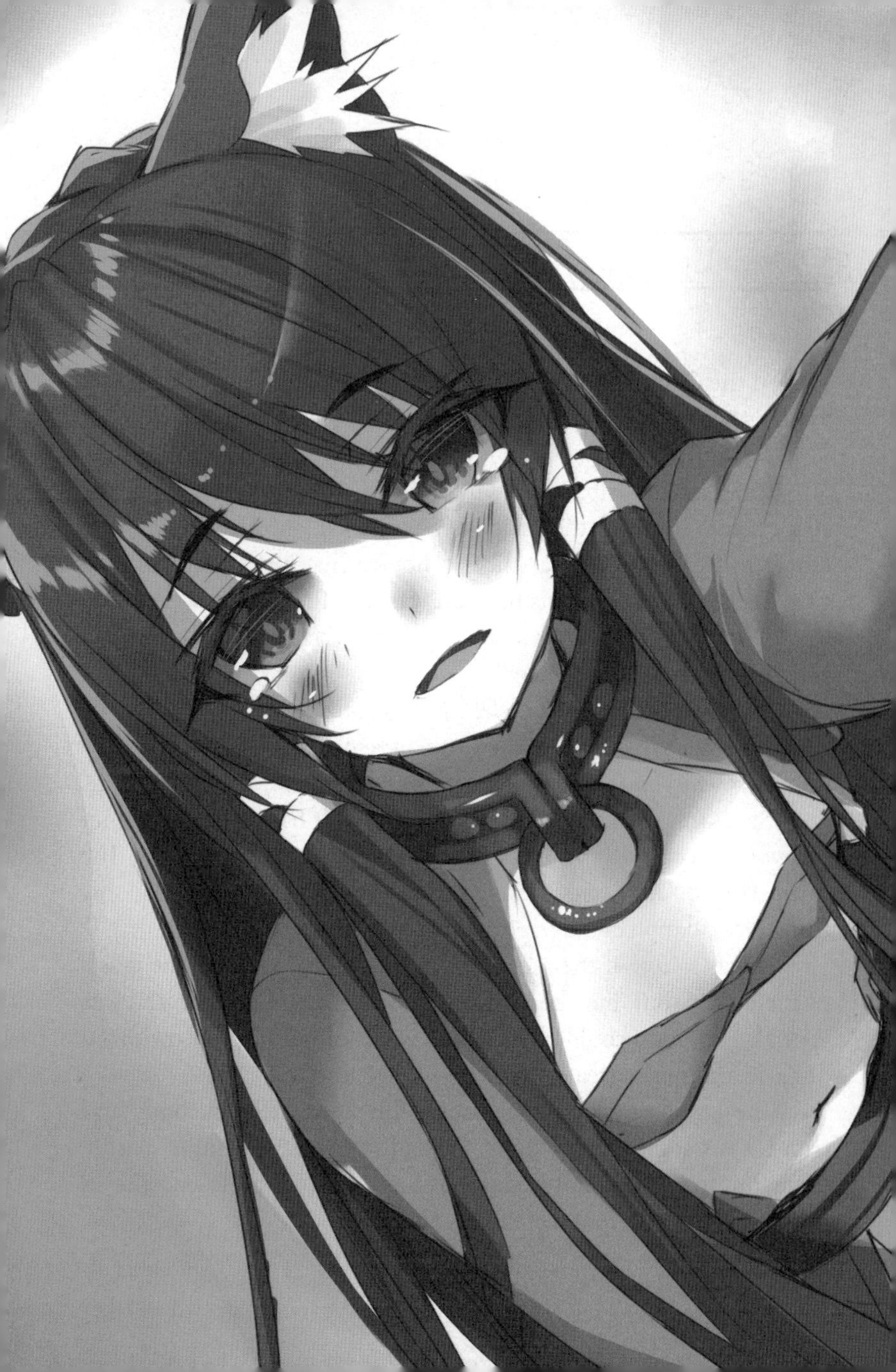

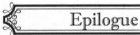

At the Gelmed Empire's invasion headquarters, Doriadanph sat with his head against the floor, clad in a casual outfit.

"I'm truly… truly sorry."

Cold sweat dripped down to the floor. Projected onto the space before him was the image of a wrinkled, old man's face… the emperor. He spoke with a voice so hoarse that just the sound of it gave one the impression his lifespan was trickling away.

"Doriadanph… Bring me the Girl of the Vessel… At all costs…!"

"At all costs, Your Grace!"

"She will be… the receptacle… for my soul…!"

"Yes! We will complete the ritual of reincarnation!"

"Hurry… You must!"

Speaking with a voice that sounded as if he was coughing up the words along with his life force, the emperor gave his decree. The image then disappeared, leaving only darkness in its wake. The only thing Doriadanph could hear was his own labored breathing.

It was said that the races' bodies could only serve as the vessel of their own soul, but the Girl of the Vessel was different, she was special. Her body could serve as the vessel of not just her own soul, but also another, a greater soul.

The emperor plotted to discard his aged, decrepit body and transfer his soul into her body. He didn't intend to simply place it there, but to have it reformed, reborn as a new life — to become an infant, with his current memories intact.

Still dressed in his everyday clothes, Doriadanph licked his lips wantingly.

As if I'd let you have her.

The emperor didn't have to be the one to use the Girl of the Vessel: Doriadanph had completed the ritual of reincarnation in secret. He may not have been as aged as the emperor, but his own body was beginning to show signs of old age and corpulence.

With the image of that black-haired Pantherian girl firmly in his mind, his eyes grew bloodshot.

I shall make good use of her.

He too wished to place his soul within her womb and be reborn as a new life.

"You won't escape, Girl of the Vessel!"

†

Concluding his conversation with the emperor through some magimatic means, Doriadanph returned to their wartime headquarters. He entered through his hidden doorway and took a seat upon his chair. Before long, there was a knock at the door.

"Come in."

One magimatic engineer entered the room at this approval. He was clad in a robe and wore a mask, so it was hard to see his facial expressions, but Doriadanph could tell he was somewhat excited.

"Magimatic Mage, sir, something incredible has happened!"

With such an introduction, Doriadanph was beginning to consider how to punish him if it were to turn out it was something insignificant.

"Speak," he prompted him to continue.

"We were holding compatibility tests on the new prisoners!"

He did order them to do that, Doriadanph recalled. Anyone with potential would be thrown into a Magimatic Sol. In nine cases out of ten, however — truthfully, the odds were even bleaker than that — they would end up being prey for the Magimatic Sols.

But in very amazing cases, there was a match. Someone who could manipulate the monsters inside those things and wield the Magimatic Sol's power.

"Was there a match?"

"Yes."

"Which Magimatic Sol was it? The teal one? Or the blue one?"

The magimatic engineer swallowed nervously.

"Goldinus of the Gold!"

Doriadanph kicked away his chair and drew on the engineer.

"Then say that sooner, you idiot!"

"C-C-Congratulations, sir!"

"If this turns out to be wrong, I'll be throwing *you* into Goldinus!"

"Please, do come and confirm it for yourself!"

They hurried to the workshop, making their way to the furthest maintenance hangar. No one usually approached it, but right now it was surrounded by a great number of magimatic engineers. Noticing Doriadanph's approach, they opened the way for him.

"Oooh…"

The unit's hatch hung open. A woman was submerged into Goldinus, still bound in chains. She wasn't consumed… She was a compatible match. The engineers were all fiddling with the woman, taking samples for checks. They drew blood, tore off hair, and collected skin tissue.

"…What about the enslavement magic?"

"Yes, we've already applied it. A Human match is incredibly rare…"

"Hmph… Her race hardly matters. People of an enemy country are disposable pawns."

As a result of the match, the woman's hair became the same color as Goldinus' armor — perfect gold, like threads of golden silk.

Doriadanph peered into the stack of documents an engineer handed him. The woman's name was…

Alicia Cristela

The girl sitting inside Goldinus opened her eyes. The engineers flew into a panic. "She's awake already?! It's too soon!" She looked around the room, her eyes burning with red.

"…So ugly."

Those were the first words Goldinus of the Gold uttered.

Afterword

This time, I've tried writing more in a 'war record' kind of style. This was the first time the story took this kind of twist, yet somehow it feels like I've written 14 volumes of this arc despite it only being one volume so far. It might be because I'm writing another series that actually is from the 'war record' genre called *Altina the Sword Princess*. It's currently being published by Famitsu Bunko, so do give it a try if you're interested.

Anyway, an afterword.

How NOT to Summon a Demon Lord's anime was incredibly well done, and I've been truly happy recently. Some developments there ended up a bit different from the novels, but I hope longtime readers can enjoy it just the same.

But let's talk about the novel for now. The Empire of Gelmed appears! I was actually planning to include them in a later volume, but it felt like "now's the time!" I figured building up too much foreshadowing would just make things boring. I hope you enjoyed it.

Next volume, I believe we'll be seeing the war with the Empire settle in one form or another, and see more about the now-blond Super Alicia and the escaped Palace Knights. I'm not sure how far the plot will go, but I intend to deliver it to you as soon as I can. Do keep supporting the series.

This volume's limited edition came included with a drama CD. I penned the script for it. I believe it came out quite well, so do give it a listen.

Some thanks, then:

To Takahiro Tsurusaki, thank you for your wonderful illustrations. To Ooishi, the designer from Afterglow, thank you for yet another volume. To my editor, Shouji, thank you for being there to help me yet again. You helped make this edition possible!

To everyone in the Kodansha light novel editorial department and everyone else involved in the publishing process. To the family and friends who supported me. And of course, to you, the readers who keep reading this series. I offer you a thank you of the highest level! Thank you very much!

Yukiya Murasaki

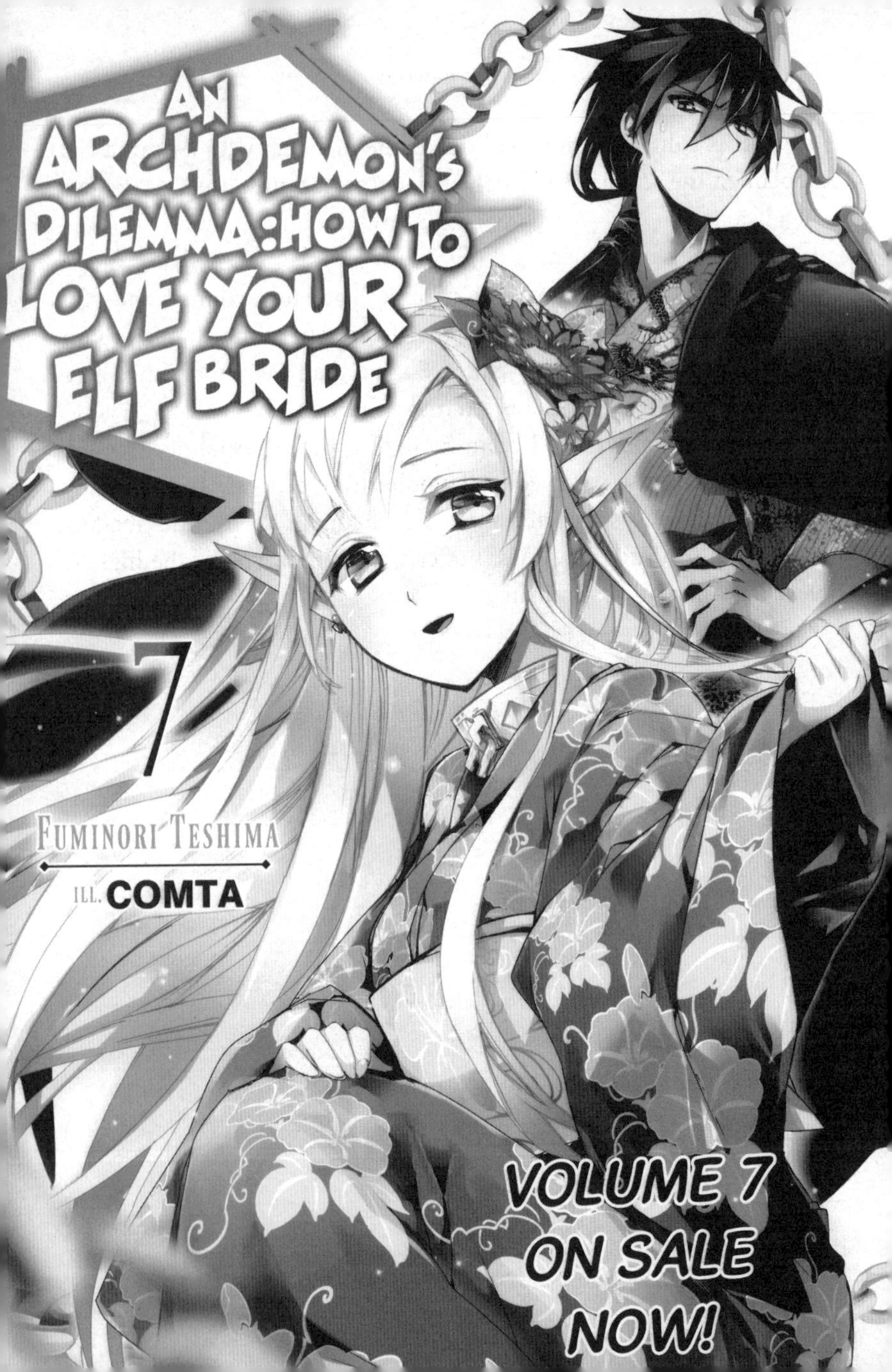

AN ARCHDEMON'S DILEMMA: HOW TO LOVE YOUR ELF BRIDE
7
FUMINORI TESHIMA
ILL. COMTA
VOLUME 7 ON SALE NOW!

In Another World With My Smartphone

12

Patora Fuyuhara

illustration・Eiji Usatsuka

VOLUME 12
ON SALE
NOW!

Sakon Kaidou

Illustrator: Taiki

VOLUME 8
ON SALE NOW!

Infinite
Dendrogram

8. The Hope They Left Behind

Ko Hiratori

Haru is back in a new
set of short stories!
On Sale Now!

JK
Haru
is a Sex Worker in
Another World
Summer

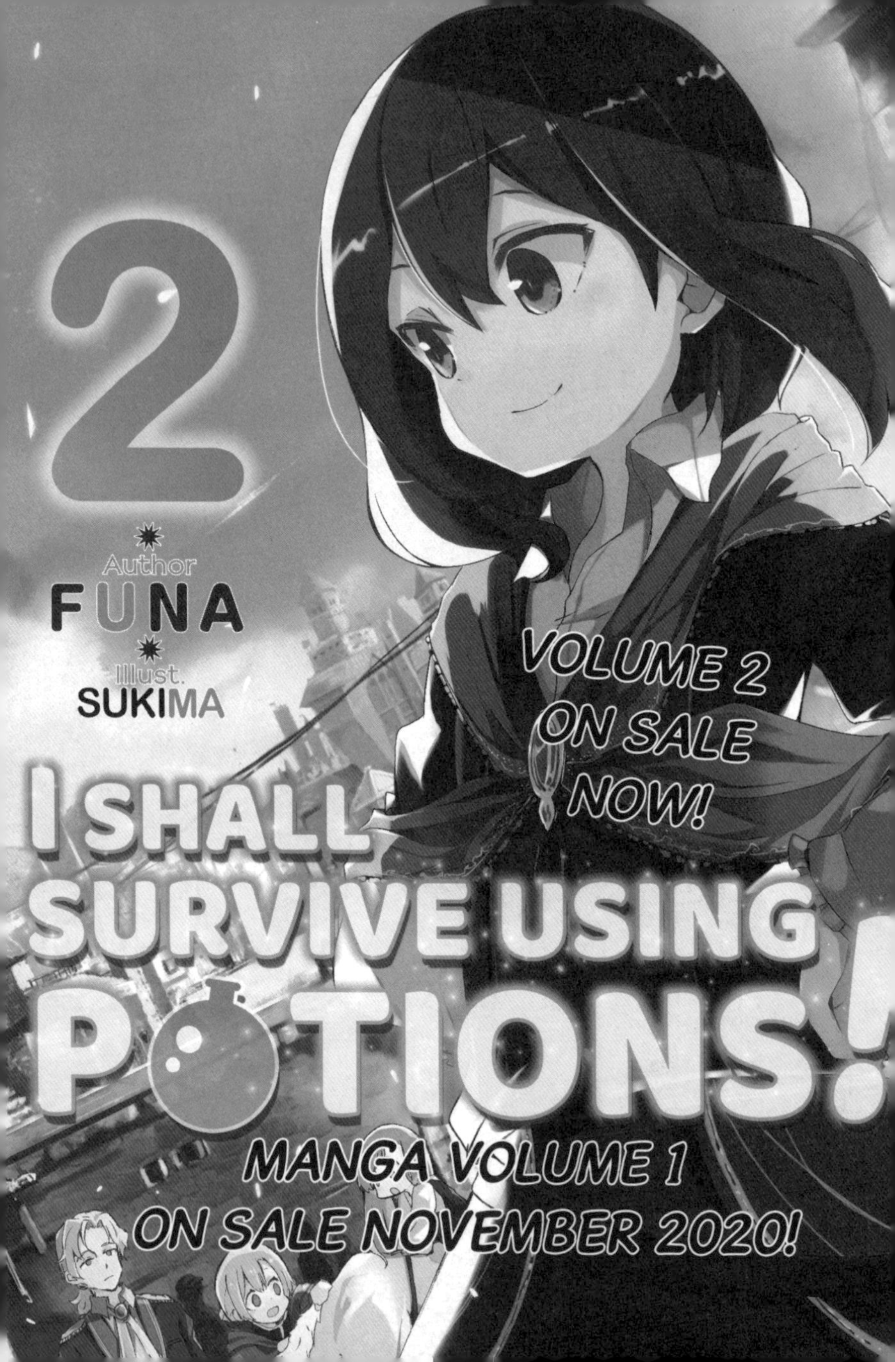
2
Author
FUNA
Illust.
SUKIMA
VOLUME 2 ON SALE NOW!
I SHALL SURVIVE USING POTIONS!
MANGA VOLUME 1 ON SALE NOVEMBER 2020!

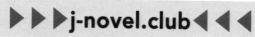

J-Novel Club Lineup

Ebook Releases Series List

Altina the Sword Princess
An Archdemon's Dilemma:
    How to Love Your Elf Bride
Arifureta Zero
Arifureta: From Commonplace
    to World's Strongest
Ascendance of a Bookworm
Beatless
Bibliophile Princess
By the Grace of the Gods
Campfire Cooking in Another World
    with My Absurd Skill
Can Someone Please Explain What's
    Going On?!
The Combat Baker and Automaton Waitress
Cooking with Wild Game
Crest of the Stars
Demon King Daimaou
Demon Lord, Retry!
Der Werwolf: The Annals of Veight
Full Metal Panic!
Grimgar of Fantasy and Ash
Her Majesty's Swarm
How a Realist Hero Rebuilt the Kingdom
How NOT to Summon a Demon Lord
I Refuse to Be Your Enemy!
I Saved Too Many Girls and Caused the
    Apocalypse
I Shall Survive Using Potions!
If It's for My Daughter, I'd Even Defeat a
    Demon Lord
In Another World With My Smartphone
Infinite Dendrogram
Infinite Stratos
Invaders of the Rokujouma!?
Isekai Rebuilding Project
JK Haru is a Sex Worker in Another World
Kobold King
Kokoro Connect
Last and First Idol
Lazy Dungeon Master
Middle-Aged Businessman, Arise in Another
    World!
Mixed Bathing in Another Dimension
My Next Life as a Villainess: All Routes Lead
    to Doom!
Otherside Picnic
Outbreak Company
Outer Ragna
Record of Wortenia War
Seirei Gensouki: Spirit Chronicles

Seriously Seeking Sister! Ultimate Vampire
    Princess Just Wants Little Sister; Plenty of
    Service Will Be Provided!
Sexiled: My Sexist Party Leader Kicked
    Me Out, So I Teamed Up With a Mythical
    Sorceress!
Sorcerous Stabber Orphen:
    The Wayward Journey
Tearmoon Empire
Teogonia
The Economics of Prophecy
The Faraway Paladin
The Greatest Magicmaster's Retirement Plan
The Holy Knight's Dark Road
The Magic in this Other World is
    Too Far Behind!
The Master of Ragnarok & Blesser of Einherjar
The Tales of Marielle Clarac
The Underdog of the Eight Greater Tribes
The Unwanted Undead Adventurer
The White Cat's Revenge as Plotted from the
    Dragon King's Lap
The World's Least Interesting Master
    Swordsman
There Was No Secret Evil-Fighting
    Organization (srsly?!), So I Made One
    MYSELF!
Welcome to Japan, Ms. Elf!

Manga Series:
A Very Fairy Apartment
An Archdemon's Dilemma:
    How to Love Your Elf Bride
Animeta!
Ascendance of a Bookworm
Cooking with Wild Game
Demon Lord, Retry!
Discommunication
How a Realist Hero Rebuilt the Kingdom
I Shall Survive Using Potions!
Infinite Dendrogram
Marginal Operation
Seirei Gensouki: Spirit Chronicles
Sorcerous Stabber Orphen:
    The Reckless Journey
Sweet Reincarnation
The Faraway Paladin
The Magic in this Other World is
    Too Far Behind!
The Master of Ragnarok & Blesser of Einherjar
The Unwanted Undead Adventurer